Racing Engine Preparation

By Waddell Wilson and Steve Smith

Editor	Steve Smith
Associate Editor	Georgiann Smith
Photos by	Steve Smith, Waddell Wilson, Georgiann Smith

ISBN #0-936834-06-4

Revised February, 1984

Published by

STEVE SMITH
AUTOSPORTS
PUBLICATIONS

P.O. Box 11631/Santa Ana, CA 92711/(714) 639-7681

WITH "GOD" YOU'RE
ALWAYS A WINNER

THE RACER'S PRAYER

Lord I pray as I race today,
Keep me safe along the way,
Not only me but others too
As they perform the jobs they do.

I know God, that in a race
I, the driver, must set the pace.

But in this race of life I pray,
Help me Lord along the way.

Although I know I am a sinner,
Help me to believe, that with
GOD you're always a winner

Bro. Bill P.O. Box 53 Gadsden, Ala. 35902

About Waddell Wilson

Waddell Wilson of Charlotte, North Carolina, has been building and tuning racing competition engines for more than 20 years. In 1963 he joined the engine department of the famed Ford Motor Company-backed Holman and Moody Inc., preparing engines for all the company's team drivers. In 1965 he was assigned exclusively to the highly successful car of Fred Lorenzen, preparing all of the engines Fred used in his many victories.

Wilson currently counts 25 major NASCAR super speedway victories to his credit, with his engines in the winning cars of such drivers as Fred Loren-zen, A.J. Foyt, David Pearson, Bobby Allison and Benny Parsons, among others. Wilson was also the exclusive engine builder for three NASCAR Grand National championship winning cars—David Pearson in 1968 and 1969, and Benny Parsons in 1973.

Approaching engine building with an analytical mind, the much-respected Wilson believes that success begins with durability. All of his work reflects this, making him one of the country's most sought-after engine builders.

A Special Thanks

We would like to extend a special thanks to all the people who helped make this book possible: **John Reed** of Reed Cams, **Murray Jensen** from Edelbrock Equipment, **Mike Urich** and **Jack Nelson** of Holley Carburetors, Grand National driver **Benny Parsons**, and GN chief mechanic **Travis Carter**.

Table of Contents

The Ignition System

The function of the ignition system essentially is to time the spark to burn the air/fuel mixture in a manner that extracts the maximum power from the engine. As the RPMs increase in the engine, this function gets tougher to accomplish because there is less time to get the job accomplished. Stock ignition components are satisfactory up to 5000 RPM, then some changes are in order.

The distributor, and its entire function within the ignition system, is very sensitive. The distributor cannot **make** horsepower, but proper attention to it and the entire system can make sure that all of the horsepower available in the engine is delivered.

DUAL POINT DISTRIBUTOR

The first change that is mandatory in any high performance engine is a dual point distributor. Replacing a single breaker point system with a dual breaker point unit increases the saturation time of the coil which is required to produce high voltage surges at increased RPMs. One of the breaker points opens the circuit while the other one closes it. This allows the dwell (saturation time) to be increased up to 8 degrees longer than any single point system can deliver. Coil saturation time begins any time either one of the sets is closed.

In any engine cylinder, there is a resistance existing between the spark plug gap which is air. As the compression in a racing engine is raised, that resistance in the gap is increased, making it increasingly harder for the spark to jump the gap. Narrowing the gap helps some, but effectively increasing the voltage of the spark is what really helps it overcome all of the resistance it encounters. The longer the dwell time (expressed in degrees of distributor cam rotation), the greater the voltage which is built up in the coil. Thus, the additional 8 degrees of distributor cam rotation with a dual point distributor gives a much hotter spark. (The distributor functions as an electric switch. To energize the coil to create a spark, the points are closed. The points open to break the circuit, creating a spark.)

BREAKER POINTS

Breaker point spring pressure is highly critical in high performance ignitions since it regulates the RPM at which "point bounce" or "float" occurs. Special points especially designed for high performance operation are mandatory. Through many years of racing experience, Wilson has found the Borg Warner high performance points to be the best. The Chevy part number is A72HP (with all centrifugal advance dual point distributors). The Ford (351C and 429) part number is A108HP (for dual point centrifugal advance distributor).

Before the points are installed in the distributor, the spring tension should be checked with a Sunnen spring tension gauge. A good racing set of

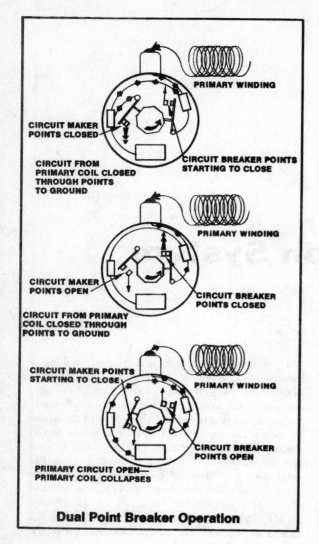

Dual Point Breaker Operation

Labels in figure:
CIRCUIT MAKER POINTS CLOSED
PRIMARY WINDING
CIRCUIT BREAKER POINTS STARTING TO CLOSE
CIRCUIT FROM PRIMARY COIL CLOSED THROUGH POINTS TO GROUND

CIRCUIT MAKER POINTS OPEN
PRIMARY WINDING
CIRCUIT BREAKER POINTS CLOSED
CIRCUIT FROM PRIMARY COIL CLOSED THROUGH POINTS TO GROUND

CIRCUIT MAKER POINTS STARTING TO CLOSE
PRIMARY WINDING
CIRCUIT BREAKER POINTS OPEN
PRIMARY CIRCUIT OPEN— PRIMARY COIL COLLAPSES

points should have at least 40 ounces of tension on this gauge.

With these heavy duty spring points operating at a high RPM, there is a problem of wear on the point rubbing block. As this rubbing block wears, dwell angle will change. (As the point gap closes up, the timing retards.) A frequent check of this wear should be made. Point gapping should be a regular routine maintenance check.

A good lubricant on the distributor cam will help hold down the wear factor. First, make sure the cam is clean. Apply a light coating of Mallory distributor cam lube. Too much lube on the cam could cause the excess to fly off and become lodged on the breaker point contact surfaces, resulting in burnt points.

We have seen some people try to use Vaseline as a distributor cam lubricant. Vaseline breaks down from heat very rapidly and is ineffective as a lube here. Various types of chassis lube are also not desirable for use on this cam because they may be too heavy or be abrasive to the cam.

THE CONDENSER

The condenser has two major functions in the ignition system. First, it prevents excessive arcing across the points when they begin to open. Second, it helps cause a rapid and sudden collapse of the ignition coil magnetic field, which induces in the secondary circuit a high voltage impulse.

It is vitally important that the condenser be matched to the breaker point set and ignition system for which it is being installed. A condenser is not just a condenser. The units are built in varying amounts of capacity, all the way from .18 to .25 microfarads. So when replacing and installing the Borg Warner points, be sure to install their

The typical automotive ignition circuit [below] begins with the primary circuit, left, when the ignition switch is activated, joining the flow of electricity from the battery to the coil. It passes all through the primary windings of the coil and exits to the points. The points act as a switch, controlling the magnetizing of the coil and the induction in the secondary windings. When the points open, the magnetic field collapses and current flows from the secondary windings, beginning the secondary circuit [right]. The current flows from the tower of the coil to the distributor rotor. Everything is timed so that everytime the points open, the rotor contacts a spark plug wire post in the cap, sending voltage through the wire to create a spark at the plug.

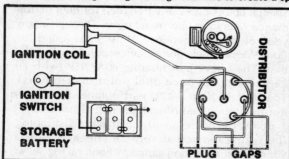

IGNITION COIL
IGNITION SWITCH
STORAGE BATTERY
DISTRIBUTOR
PLUG GAPS

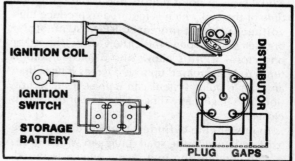

IGNITION COIL
IGNITION SWITCH
STORAGE BATTERY
DISTRIBUTOR
PLUG GAPS

matching condenser. The Chevy condenser part number is G102HP and the Ford part number is G111HP (these are both for the dual point centrifugal advance distributors for which breaker point part numbers were given).

The capacity of the condenser affects breaker point pitting (or the transfer of material from one point to the other). If the material collects on the positive side of the points (the breaker lever arm), the condenser is under capacity and a higher capacity condenser should be used. If the material collects on the negative side (the contact support of the points set), the condenser is over capacity.

Many times an ignition problem can be diagnosed as a bad condenser. Beware! A very common problem is a poor ground contact. Be sure the contact is always absolutely clean and tight.

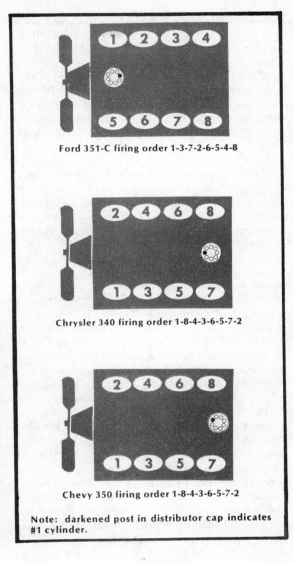

Ford 351-C firing order 1-3-7-2-6-5-4-8

Chrysler 340 firing order 1-8-4-3-6-5-7-2

Chevy 350 firing order 1-8-4-3-6-5-7-2

Note: darkened post in distributor cap indicates #1 cylinder.

The worst place for a coil is in the hot engine compartment. In this position it is also subject to vibration.

THE COIL

The coil is basically a transformer, converting 12 volts which are fed into it to anywhere from

This coil and ballast resistor has been placed out of the heat of the engine compartment to preserve the life of the coil.

25,000 to 40,000 volts output. This output goes through the high tension wire back to the distributor where it is distributed by the rotor to the spark plugs.

Why so many volts of output? Because that is what is required inside the engine cylinder to make the spark jump from the center electrode to the ground electrode of the plug. And the greater the cylinder compression and the faster the engine RPM, the greater the voltage required to make the jump.

The interior of the coil consists of two coiled windings of wire. One is the primary winding, the other is the secondary winding. When the breaker points are closed, low voltage current is fed into the primary winding. The high amperage current entering the primary windings completely surrounds the secondary windings with a very strong magnetic field which produces an electric current in the secondary by a phenomenon called induction. The greater number of turns in the secondary winding multiplies the voltage into the greater amount. This is why a longer dwell time is desired. It gives this secondary voltage more time to be built up. At high RPMs, the points are only closed for a short period which gives the coil less time to become saturated with battery current. The result is less current flowing out to the plugs.

The two greatest enemies of the coil are heat and vibration. For this reason, the best place on a race car to mount the coil is through the firewall so the coil body is exposed to the rush of incoming air through the cowl air intake area.

A coil which is in top operational shape is mandatory for a high performance engine. But one of the high cost high performance coils is not necessarily required. For the money, the best buy is stock parts. Use the GM (Delco) part number 1115207 coil or the Ford part number D4AZ-12029A. For MoPar cars with dual point distributors, use coil part number P3690560. Many of the after-market coils are advertised to deliver 40,000 to 50,000 volts. In many case, this excessive voltage could prove to be more of a problem than a help.

THE ADVANCE MECHANISM

The function of any advance mechanism on a distributor is to fire the air/fuel mixture earlier as the engine revs faster. Almost all stock distributors use a combination system of vacuum and centrifugal advance. But because vacuum advance is only effective in part throttle operation, only centrifugal advance mechanisms are used on dual point distributors for racing. Vacuum advance has no place in high performance applications.

The centrifugal advance works by use of weights and springs. As centrifugal force increases (the distributor shaft is rotating faster), the weights overcome the spring tension which locates them and manually rotate the distributor into a more advanced operation range to fire the air/fuel mixture sooner BTDC.

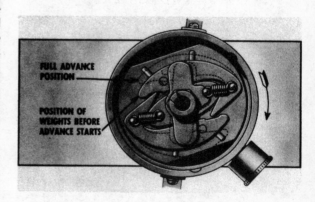

Below, the Ford 351-C distributor advance mechanism.

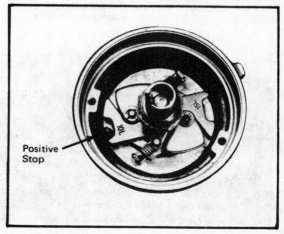

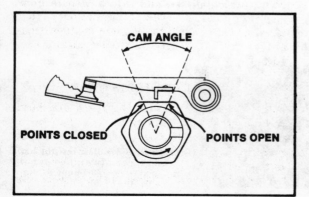

The weight of the advance weights is what determines the amount of advance. The heavier the weights, the more the advance. The tension of the springs which locate the weights is what determines the rate at which the weights advance the distributor. The softer the spring rate, the quicker the advance.

There are a number of companies which supply advance weight and spring kits which can be used to alter the advance curve. Mr. Gasket Company has kits #925A for the GM distributors (925B for MoPar distributors, and 925D for Fords, which are preferred by Wilson for the GM distributor). Jack Cotten Ignitions has a kit for all three makers (4925A for GM, 4925B for Chrysler cars and 4925D for Fords). Chrysler also produces their own kit for the 340 distributor, part number P2932675.

It is important that the advance mechanism be kept lightly oiled with a lightweight oil. This prevents rust which could make it stick or hang up.

FORD CENTRIFUGAL ADVANCE

The Ford centrifugal advance curve on its dual point distributors can be altered by bending the spring posts. The centrifugal advance plate stop must be moved so it is against the "10L" marking, on the plate. Bend the outer clip of the primary spring outward 1/8". This set-up will start the advance at 1000 RPM and have 12 degrees total advance in at 3500 RPM. The neoprene shock absorber on the stop must be removed for everything to work right.

THE ADVANCE CURVE

The advance curve on all stock car racing engines, big block or small block, should be the same whether a dual point or electronic ignition system is being used.

The total advance should be 38°, which should all be in by 3500 RPM. The 38° is a maximum for oval track engines (which have 12 or 12.5 to 1 compression). With 10 or 10.5 to 1 compression, the engine can tolerate as much as 42° total advance. But if you run this much advance, be sure to check the plugs for signs of detonation. On tracks such as Daytona, where wide-open throttle operation is encountered, a minimum of 36° total advance must be used. Any more than this will lead to detonation and a loss of horsepower. The 3500 RPM range is a good point at which to have all the advance in, although in some situations it just is not possible. In these cases, 4000 RPM should be the maximum tolerable range.

If the full advance is in before 3000 RPM, the engine is going to suffer from detonation as it accelerates up to this range. This will knock the wrist pins out and cause higher cylinder temperature. The full advance should be in by 4000 RPM at the maximum, or it will become increasingly dangerous to check the advance with a timing light when the engine is revving very high.

The advance curve should start no earlier than 1000 RPM, with 1200 RPM being the optimum. This will yield a smoother running engine at idle and it will also make it possible to set the timing at the crankshaft at idle before the advance curve starts.

The total spark advance is a combination of the advance mechanism in the distributor and the advance set with the timing light at the crankshaft. Remember the distributor speed is one-half the crankshaft speed, so to find total advance, double the full advance of the distributor, then subtract this from 38°. The amount which is left is the amount of advance BTDC which will be set at the crankshaft.

For example, if the distributor advance is 12° maximum, double this. It will equal 24°. Subtract 24° from 38° and the remainder is 14°. So the engine timing would then be set at 14° advance. To check the total advance, put a 38° mark on the damper. Then run the engine up to 4000 RPM and the pointer should show 0 on the damper.

Because it is sometimes difficult to regulate the weights which control the centrifugal advance, the tolerance for the distributor advance is anywhere between 9° and 13°. The optimum, however, is 11° or 12°.

Because of the longer duration and overlap of the camshafts used in high performance engines, these engines need at least 14° to 16° advance at idle. So this dictates that the distributor advance not be more than 12°.

Engines which have hemi-shaped cylinder heads do not require as much timing advance as wedge engines, because the spark flame does not have to travel as far to reach the air/fuel mixture. Hemi engines generally take 32° to 34° total timing advance.

THE DISTRIBUTOR MACHINE

It is an absolute must to check any distributor to be used in a racing engine on a distributor machine. This is the only way to set one up correctly, and be able to know what to expect out of the distributor.

First, check the distributor for shaft wear. The

next check should be for a bent shaft, but this is very easy to detect. As soon as the distributor is bolted into the machine, and it is turned on, a bent shaft will show itself as a bad wobble. As the machine RPMs are increased, a bent shaft will cause enough vibration to make it difficult to keep the distributor in the machine.

The next check to make on the distributor machine is point resistance. The machine has a scale that shows either good or bad and a selector switch to connect the scale to the points. The resistance should show in the good range if the points are new or in good condition. If it shows in the bad range, the points are incorrectly installed, misaligned or there is a loose ground or lead wire. If the points are not new, burnt points also cause the meter to show in the bad range. The points need to be closed to perform this test.

To check the resistance of the points with a dual point distributor, block one set of points with a piece of clean paper or cardboard while the other one is being tested.

While checking for the resistance, look to see if the contact set is slightly misaligned or bent. **Gently** work with the contact arm to get the alignment of the faces back together straight. Be careful not to force the breaker arm too much. A bent arm frequently causes it to break in half while running at high RPMs.

The next step is the dwell adjustment. The dwell or cam angle is the number of degrees of distributor cam rotation during which the contact points remain closed. Specifications for dwell are also given in distance of point gap opening. These two specifications work together—as the cam dwell degrees increase, the point gap opening is decreased.

The dwell specifications required for the Chevrolet dual point distributors is 29° on each set of points and 31° total when both sets of points are run together.

The Ford dwell specifications for the dual point distributor is 24° on each set of points and a 32° total with both sets running together. If the individual breaker sets are correct, the total dwell falls in place automatically.

When the dwell is being set for a dual point distributor, each set of points must be treated separately. Use a piece of clean, lint-free white paper to block one set of points while the other one is being adjusted. The white paper is important because it allows you to instantly see if the point contact surfaces are clean.

After installing new points in a distributor, readjust the dwell angle after some break-in time on the engine. The initial break-in of the rubbing block surface on the points will always change the setting somewhat.

After the dwell has been set on the distributor, run the distributor past 4000 engine RPM at least three times and decelerate it to see if the dwell setting changes any. It shouldn't. Then run the distributor past the maximum engine RPM the engine is expected to encounter and check for any point bounce.

The final check on the distributor machine is for spark scatter. According to theory and design, all eight cylinders should be fired by the distributor at the same degree. But because of wear and manufacturing tolerances, it does not always work

Sun distributor machine

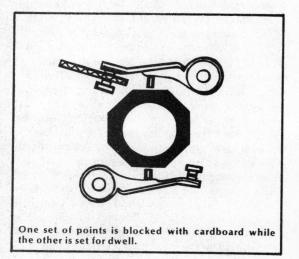

One set of points is blocked with cardboard while the other is set for dwell.

out that way. The maximum allowable tolerance for a high performance engine should be 2°. If there is any more than this, change the distributor cam. One after-market distributor we tested while writing this book advanced one plug 2½°, retarded one 2°, and varied all the others 1°-1½°. This distributor will never develop the maximum potential horsepower in the engine in which it is installed.

DISTRIBUTOR MAINTENANCE

No matter what type of distributor system you have on your car, dirt is an enemy of it. Periodically disassemble and clean the distributor. Dirt can cause irregularity in timing, sticky advance mechanism and poor lubrication. If your car is operating on a track where sand or dust is prevalent, use a "dum dum" type of pliable sealer under the distributor cap sealing edge to be certain none of the dirt gets in.

Check the manufacturer's service manual which covers the brand of distributor you are using regarding the lubrication procedure. The periodic oiling is vital, but each distributor is treated differently. Check yours to be sure.

THE DELCO DUAL POINT DISTRIBUTOR

The best GM dual point distributor is part number 1110891. It is listed in the parts book as a high performance option for the 1957 Corvette. It comes with centrifugal advance only and the curve is correct already so no spring or weight changes are necessary. It also checks out on the distributor machine to have almost zero spark scatter. This unit does not have mechanical tach

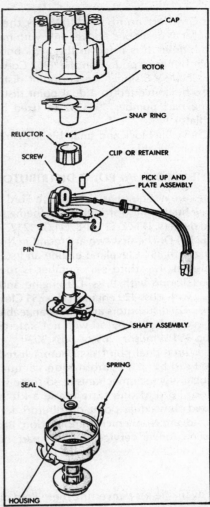

Above, the drawing illustrates the Chrysler electronic ignition system.

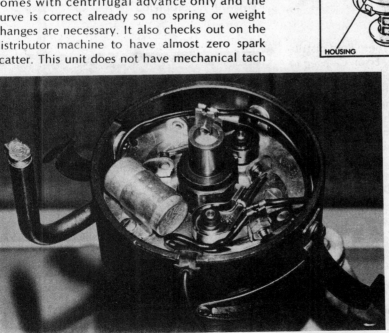

The 1957 Corvette version of the GM Delco dual point distributor.

drive.

The GM part number 1110985 is the same distributor as described above, only with mechanical tach drive. It is listed in the parts book as a high performance option on the 1962 Corvette.

Any Chevy V-8 single breaker point distributor can also be converted to a dual point distributor by using part number 1953752 (a fixed breaker point plate).

All Chevy big block and small block distributors are interchangeable.

THE FORD DUAL POINT DISTRIBUTOR

Things are not quite as easy with a Ford. There are three dual point distributors still being service by Ford dealers: D1ZZ 12127-E, D1ZZ 12127-G and C9ZZ 12127-D. The first two are found in the 1971 Mustang with 351 Cleveland engine and standard transmission. The third part number is found in the 1969 Torino with Boss 429 engine and 1969 Mustang with Boss 429 engine. (The 351 Cleveland and Boss 429 distributors are interchangeable. The 351 Cleveland distributor will not interchange with the 351 Windsor, 289 or Boss 302.)

These three dual point distributors listed here for the Ford have a combination vacuum and centrifugal advance mechanism, so some work is required. Ford at one time made a kit which converted these dual point distributors for centrifugal advance-only racing application. But Ford dealers no longer service this kit, part number D1AZ-12A-132-A.

Also available for converting these Ford distributors is a conversion kit from Sig Erson Cams (part number 913032). It includes the fixed breaker point plate and advance weights and springs.

Other options available for the Ford distributor are complete after-market distributors. Mr. Gasket Company makes one (part number 4232 for the 351 Cleveland) and Mallory makes one (part number YL567HP for the 351C).

THE MOPAR DUAL POINT DISTRIBUTOR

There are dual point distributors for the MoPar 340 engine if you do not desire to use the MoPar race-proven electronic ignition system.

The dual point distributor is part number 3438318. It has centrifugal and vacuum advance. Remove the vacuum mechanism and plug the housing hole. Braze the advance plate to the solid mounting plate. Use any of the advance curve

modification kits mentioned earlier. Install Borg Warner points part number A99 HP and condenser part number G122 HP.

ELECTRONIC IGNITION SYSTEMS

As the Detroit auto makers switch over more and more to the electronic ignition systems on passenger cars, these systems are also becoming more common on high performance racing vehicles

Basically there are two types of systems being employed as electronic ignition. The first uses a magnetic pulse trigger to fire the system instead of points opening and closing. A reluctor replaces the distributor cam and rotates past a stationary magnetic pickup pole. This triggers the spark through an electronic amplifying circuit.

The second type of system has an infra-red light beam which is interrupted by a rotating light chopper. When the light beam is broken the spark is triggered into an electronic amplifier circuit.

What these systems offer is a hotter primary current (which would burn regular breaker points) and a longer coil saturation time to produce a hotter spark. The other advantage is never having to replace points and condensers nor having to set the point dwell.

In any of these systems, the electronic amplifying circuit is the critical part. If you are going to install one on your car, be sure you know the RPM capability of the circuit. Some units only function as high as 5000 RPM, while others go up to 8500 RPM with no problem.

If you are going to be competing in any long distance races, a good idea for your ignition is to have an auxiliary amplifier unit [for transistor ignitions]. If one unit gives up, just plug into next.

MOPAR ELECTRONIC IGNITION

The MoPar electronic ignition system is the magnetic pulse system. To install it on a 340 engine, use package #P3690422 (includes a mechanical drive tach—without the mechanical drive tach use part number P3690426). The kit consists of a competition-curved distributor (P3690200 with mechanical tach drive), electronic control box number P3690256 (this is the amplifying circuit), wiring harness (P3690152) and ballast resistor (P3656199). You will also need a high output coil, part number P3690560.

The stock MoPar distributor and oil pump drive shaft is not adequate for high performance engines, so a heavy duty driveshaft and gear assembly (part number P3690715) should be used.

DELCO ELECTRONIC IGNITION

A more reliable—but more expensive— Chevy ignition system is the Delco magnetically triggered electronic ignition system. The distributor is part number 1111263 (a ball bearing, centrifugal advance unit with mechanical tach drive). Use amplifier part number 3997782 (this includes the special high output coil, amplifier unit and wire and harness assembly). Be sure to take the amplifier back plate off and use electronic potting compound (or silicone caulking) inside the unit to soak up vibrations.

Any point-type Chevy distributor can be converted to a magnetic pulse-type by installing the stationary and rotating pieces inside (part numbers 1964272 and 1960779), and use with amplifier unit 3997782.

BORG WARNER ELECTRONIC IGNITION

Borg Warner makes a very good infra-red light type of electronic ignition system. And its amplifying circuit is guaranteed up to 10,000 RPMs. For Chevies use their part number EI-1. For Fords, use part number EI-3. Both of these part numbers are for the complete package which includes the trigger light, light chopper, wire harness and control box. Installation is easy and instructions are included. For high performance engines, Borg Warner recommends that the standard ignition's resistor be replaced with Borg Warner number RU12 resistor.

An increasing number of serious engine builders are using the Autotronics MSD (Multiple Spark Discharge) system to augment whatever distributor assembly they prefer.

CAPACITOR DISCHARGE IGNITION

The capacitor discharge ignition is basically an add-on circuit to be used with a breaker point-type of ignition system. Its purpose is to reduce the current flowing through the point contact surfaces for longer point life, then transform the primary current into a hotter secondary current for a hotter spark. The RPM capability of the circuit in these systems is also very critical. High energy build-up during a very short time is the beauty of the capacitor discharge system, allowing it to successfully fire even wide-gapped, fouled plugs at high RPM.

SPARK PLUGS

Very often the words "hot" and "cold", when used in reference to spark plug heat ranges, are a source of confusion. Normally, a hot plug is used in a low horsepower, cold engine, and a cold plug is used in a high horsepower, hot engine.

The terms hot and cold actually refer to a plug's thermal characteristics, or heat rating. More specifically, these terms refer to the plug's ability to transfer heat from its firing end into the engine's cylinder head.

A cold heat range plug transfers heat quite rapidly from its firing end and is used to avoid overheating where the combustion chamber temperatures are relatively high. A hot heat range plug has a much slower rate of heat transfer and will avoid fouling where combustion chamber temperatures get in the low range.

The length of the core nose and the electrode alloy material are the primary factors in establishing the heat range of a particular spark plug design, according to Champion Spark Plug Co. Hot plugs have longer insulator noses with longer heat transfer paths. Cold plugs have shorter insulator nose lengths and thus allow them to transfer heat more rapidly.

Since the insulator tip is usually the hottest part of the spark plug, its temperature can be related to preignition and fouling. In non-supercharged gasoline burning 4-cycle engines, preignition is likely to occur if anything in the combustion chamber exceeds 1750°F. Fouling, or shorting of the plug due to carbon, is likely to occur if its insulator tip temperature drops to approximately 600°F. The ideal combustion chamber operation temperature for a racing engine is 1350°F.

HEAT RANGE SELECTION

Racing engines develop very high combustion temperatures. "Street" type spark plugs cannot survive this thermal environment, especially when

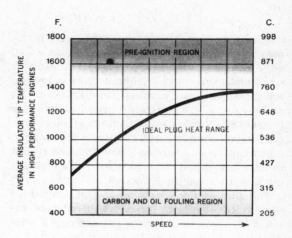

sustaining full power operation. Consequently, racing plugs have a colder heat range. Preliminary heat range selection tailors the plug to the cylinder pressure and heat which the engine basically develops, but the final heat range selection is more precise when the nature of the course, the weather and the engine induction system are considered.

Heat range selection consists of choosing a plug which will keep the engine balanced thermally between fouling and preignition at all engine RPM ranges and course conditions.

Proper heat range selection should position the plug's operating temperature well below the preignition zone as any abnormalities in timing or carburetion during the race could send the engine into preignition, burning the plugs or severely damaging the engine.

There are five very important factors which

Champion Spark Plug Identification System

Basic Heat Range Numbers

Example:

| N | – | 57 | R |

All Champion spark plug numbers fit into *four* categories defining *application* and *heat range*.

	1	Cold	Cold	51	
Automotive & Hi-Performance	Thru	↕	↕	Thru	... Racing
	25	Hot	Hot	75	
Aircraft ...	26	Cold	Cold	76	Special & Racing
	Thru	↕	↕	Thru	
	50	Hot	Hot	99	

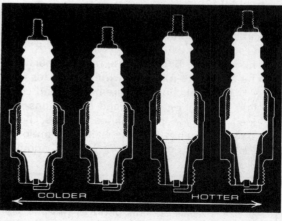

Drawing shows how plug size effects its heat range.

influence the heat range selection of the plug: compression ratio, spark advance timing, air/fuel mixture ratio, gasoline octane and the length of time of continuous full throttle operation. All of these factors actually influence the combustion chamber temperature, and their combination must be considered when choosing the correct plug heat range which will survive in that environment.

The higher the compression ratio, the higher the combustion chamber temperature will be. A higher compression ratio also produces a higher cylinder pressure which is trying to "quench" the spark.

Spark advance timing has one of the greatest effects on spark plug temperature. The greater the advance BTDC, the higher the combustion chamber temperature and cylinder pressure. Too great a spark advance can lead to detonation.

Air/fuel mixture ratio means "rich" or "lean" in mixture. A lean mixture has a comparatively large volume of air in relation to the fuel volume. A rich mixture is one with a small volume of air in relation to the fuel volume.

Lean mixtures can be dangerous, inviting pre-ignition and detonation because they burn more slowly and require a longer time to conduct heat away from the combustion chamber, plugs and piston crown.

Finding the best mixture is a delicate problem at best. Usually the best peak horsepower can be found when the mixture is tending toward lean, but when it is being run, a constant check should be made on the plugs to see if any damage is being done in the cylinder.

Although some power is sacrificed, a slightly rich mixture offers a margin of safety because it absorbs heat from the air and cylinder surfaces, offers detonation protection at full throttle and satisfies the leanest cylinder.

If you are ever in doubt as to proper jetting (when an overlean condition is suspected), always enrichen. This will keep cylinder temperatures out of the critical range.

Gasoline octane rating makes a difference in the burning rate of the fuel. The lower the octane, the quicker the detonation and preignition will occur.

How long the engine is in full throttle operation sometimes makes a change in heat range necessary. Tracks having long straightaways or courses with high-banked, high-speed turns generally require colder plugs than a short track where the length of full throttle operation is short. For example, the same car running on three different tracks might require a Champion BL-57 at Daytona, a BL-60 at Rockingham and a BL-3 at a half-mile track with flat, sharp turns.

GAP SIZES

Wide spark plug gaps in a high speed racing engine can invite a high speed miss due to a decreased coil saturation time. Wide gaps can also stress coils and cause ignition harness breakdown.

In stock car racing engines with compression ratios anywhere from 10 to 1 to 12.5 to 1, the plug gap should be between .022" and .025".

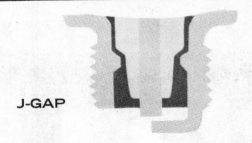

J-GAP

A conventional automotive type gap slightly modified . . . side electrode extends midway to the center electrode . . . gap design requires less firing voltage at high RPM . . . also protects from ingested particles wedging between gap and shorting out plug. Plug design offers good fouling protection and excellent performance in many racing applications.

The J and Y gaps are the only two gap styles to consider other than the regular gap.

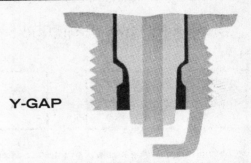

Y-GAP

Commonly used in overhead-valve racing engines where sufficient physical clearance exists between piston or valves. Plug heat range characteristics are slightly different from other plugs as incoming fuel charge cools insulator tip at high speed . . . long tip runs hotter at lower speeds . . . an effective plug in wedge type combustion chambers . . . this design offers excellent fouling protection from rich mixture conditions . . . when converting to this design from retracted or regular gap plugs, ignition timing may have to be retarded slightly . . . plug design is not recommended for maximum output engines, highly supercharged, or high percentage nitro-burners.

Extremely wide gaps, even when being fired by a capacitive discharge system, are not wise because an ignition system output weakness developed during a race could cause the ignition to completely fail.

DETONATION AND PREIGNITION

Detonation is an uncontrolled burning of the fuel. A smooth flame front does not occur. Detonation is a violent collision of flame fronts within the cylinder occurring after the spark plug has fired. It is a physical shock in the chamber.

Detonation is not detected in practice or competition because its audible sound (a "ping") is drowned out by the roar of open exhausts. A racing engine will not perform at its peak when in detonation. A racing engine cannot survive very long even in a mild state of detonation, as the physical and thermal stresses inflict progressive damage to parts such as pistons, plugs, rods and bearings.

Detonation can lead to preignition. When preignition occurs, a spark is not required to ignite the fuel. Rather, a part within the combustion chamber reaches the point of incandescence and the fuel simply ignites without the aid of a spark. As no orderly firing sequence occurs, the engine is out of time.

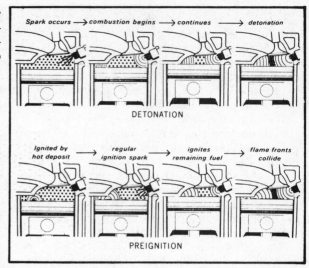

Preignition destroys the engine by heat, not by mechanical shock. The searing increase in heat can cause a piston to melt, seize, break or the entire engine to blow.

Providing the plug heat range is correct, a piston is the most vulnerable part of the engine. It takes heat over the full surface of its crown but can pass heat only at its circumference to the piston rings which transfer the heat to the thin oil film on the cylinder wall.

Preignition will melt a hole in the top of a piston, whereas detonation will hammer a hole in the top of it. As soon as either case is suspected in an engine, the mixture should be richened or the timing should be retarded.

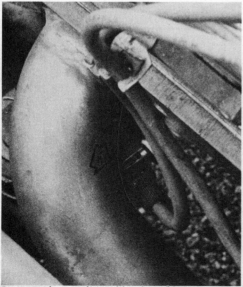

Beware of a condition like this. The plug electrode and wiring are within ¼ " of the header tube, and is shorted out by grounding across to the header.

If you want to keep all the ignitions wiring running correctly and in place, use wire looms with protective rubber grommets such as this. The loom keeps the wires separated so voltage cannot jump from one to another, plus it keeps wires off hot headers.

Broken pistons [see arrows] reveal evidence of severe detonation.

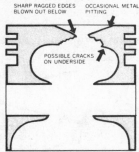

DETONATION

SHARP RAGGED EDGES BLOWN OUT BELOW

OCCASIONAL METAL PITTING

POSSIBLE CRACKS ON UNDERSIDE

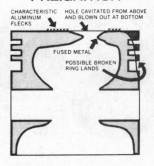

PREIGNITION

CHARACTERISTIC ALUMINUM FLECKS

HOLE CAVITATED FROM ABOVE AND BLOWN OUT AT BOTTOM

FUSED METAL

POSSIBLE BROKEN RING LANDS

READING SPARK PLUGS

There is more **potential** horsepower to be gained in cylinder temperature distribution fine tuning than any place else in the engine. And the area which gives the best indication of what is going on in the combustion chamber is spark plug coloring.

Every plug of the set removed from an engine should look alike in coloring and condition. Any difference among them is an indication that combustion chamber temperature, fuel/air ratios and fuel distribution are not the same in every cylinder, or there are other engine problems that need attention.

If differences are found in the spark plug coloring, the problems can usually be traced to one or more of the following areas:

1. Intake manifold unequal distribution
2. Ignition system weakness
3. Poor oil control
4. Weak compression
5. Unequal valve timing
6. Spark scatter
7. Cooling system problems

You may find the cylinder temperatures varying to such an extreme among the cylinders that it would require two different spark plug heat ranges to successfully balance the engine. If such differences are found, the conditions which cause this must be diagnosed and corrected. An engine is not going to put out at its maximum potential like this.

New spark plugs will take at least two to three laps, at a minimum, to color in. The spark plug readings must be taken after the engine has operated at its maximum power output. This means the ignition must be shut off at the end of a straightaway, and then coast the car into the pits. If the car is decelerated into the pits under its own power, the true spark plug coloring will be shaded or erased and faulty reading will occur.

The photos of common spark plug readings (shown here courtesy of Champion Spark Plugs) will give you an indication of what to look for. Use a Champion Sparkplug Viewer to get a true indication of what the plugs "say." It lights and magnifies the plugs.

In addition to the illustrations of plug conditions shown here, there are two more important things to look for. First, be aware that the flat ring around the bottom of the porcelain insulator is the first area to color on new plugs (because this is the area that cools last). This is where you should look for signs of proper fuel distribution. The ring

READING RACING SPARK PLUGS

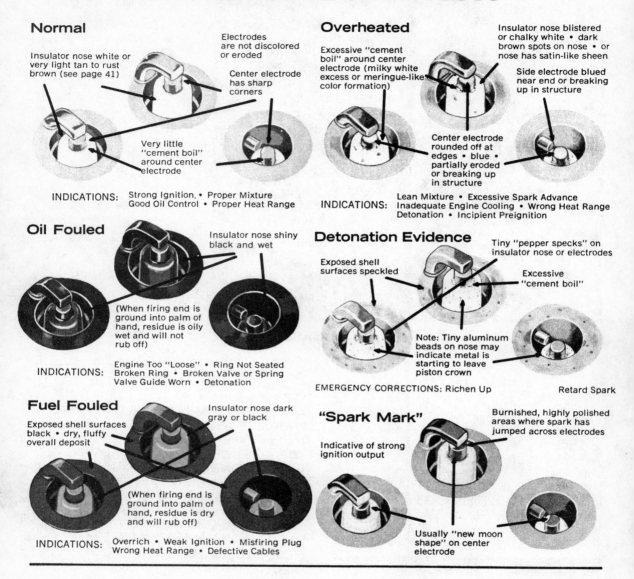

Normal

Insulator nose white or very light tan to rust brown (see page 41)

Electrodes are not discolored or eroded

Center electrode has sharp corners

Very little "cement boil" around center electrode

INDICATIONS: Strong Ignition • Proper Mixture Good Oil Control • Proper Heat Range

Overheated

Excessive "cement boil" around center electrode (milky white excess or meringue-like color formation)

Insulator nose blistered or chalky white • dark brown spots on nose • or nose has satin-like sheen

Side electrode blued near end or breaking up in structure

Center electrode rounded off at edges • blue • partially eroded or breaking up in structure

INDICATIONS: Lean Mixture • Excessive Spark Advance Inadequate Engine Cooling • Wrong Heat Range Detonation • Incipient Preignition

Oil Fouled

Insulator nose shiny black and wet

(When firing end is ground into palm of hand, residue is oily wet and will not rub off)

INDICATIONS: Engine Too "Loose" • Ring Not Seated Broken Ring • Broken Valve or Spring Valve Guide Worn • Detonation

Detonation Evidence

Exposed shell surfaces speckled

Tiny "pepper specks" on insulator nose or electrodes

Excessive "cement boil"

Note: Tiny aluminum beads on nose may indicate metal is starting to leave piston crown

EMERGENCY CORRECTIONS: Richen Up   Retard Spark

Fuel Fouled

Exposed shell surfaces black • dry, fluffy overall deposit

Insulator nose dark gray or black

(When firing end is ground into palm of hand, residue is dry and will rub off)

INDICATIONS: Overrich • Weak Ignition • Misfiring Plug Wrong Heat Range • Defective Cables

"Spark Mark"

Indicative of strong ignition output

Burnished, highly polished areas where spark has jumped across electrodes

Usually "new moon shape" on center electrode

---

should be a light tan, slightly earthy color. If it is a light gray or off white, the mixture is too lean. If the ring is medium to dark gray, the mixture is too lean.

The top ring on the outside of the plug (to which the ground electrode is connected) can tell you if the plug has been torqued too tightly. If the torque has been too tight, this ring will have been protruding too far into the combustion chamber and it will be shiny or have a significant difference in color from one side of the plug to the other.

The Crankshaft

It would seem as though there would be little to do to a crankshaft but to check it for straightness and lay it in the engine. Not so. No matter how well the manufacturers claim they are making their cranks, there is a lot which can be done to improve the reliability and durability of the crankshaft in a high performance engine.

The first thing to realize about reliability is that cast iron cranks just seem to be lacking in this department, except for one crank. The best

crank to use at all times is a forged steel one. All manufacturers have them available for all engines commonly being used in racing applications, except for the Ford 351-C. All that is available from Ford is a nodular iron crank, which we may point out, has been used quite successfully for several years by Bud Moore, the Wood Brothers and others competing with 351-Clevelands. However, if you want the forged steel variety for your Ford, it is available from Moldex Tool Co. It does sell at

A large screwdriver is inserted against crank throw to drive crank rearward against thrust bearing. This is how crank end play is measured. The dial indicator on end of crank measures amount of end play.

a premium price. The regular Ford 351-C nodular iron crank is part number DIZZ 6303-A.

The Chevrolet 350 forged steel crank, available from your Chevy dealer, is part number 3941184 Chevrolet also makes available a semi-finished version of this crank in case you want to take it to a crankshaft specialty company and have the stroke altered. It is available under part number 3997748.

For the MoPar 340 engines, there are two different forged steel cranks available. The first is the regular production (1968-1972) crankshaft, part number 2843885. It has a 6-bolt rear flange, which is standard for the 340 engines. A high performance forged steel crank is also available under part number P3690905. This crank has an 8-bolt rear flange, which is the hemi-engine pattern. Both of these cranks have the stock 3.31-inch stroke. For NASCAR Grand National racing, Moldex Tool

Above, Wilson uses a ratchet micrometer to measure crank journal diameter. Measurements have to be taken twice to eliminate errors created by the operator's hand warming the metal.

Notice smooth radiused fillets on crank [see arrow]. The larger the radius, the lesser the chance of crankshaft cracking in this highly stressed area. Notice how the cross-drilled oil hole openings have been chamfered and radiused.

The thrust bearing is sanded on its side to gain crank end play. Be sure sand paper is on flat surface to avoid getting low spots on bearing.

A dial indicator is installed against each main journal and the crank is rotated to check for journal run-out.

Company has a special forged steel crank available which has a 3.461-inch stroke, yielding a 355 cubic inch engine without any overbore.

CLEARANCES

The desired main and rod bearing clearances for any engine being raced in an oval track or road racing situation is .0025-inch.

For crankshaft end play, use .007-inch for an oval track racing engine, and .004-inch for an engine which will be used on a road racing course where frequent shifting must be endured. The closer end play tolerance for the road racing crankshaft is to allow some wear from the frequent shifting. Crankshaft end play is designed to allow hot oil to escape out of the thrust bearing. Too little clearance will disrupt constant flow of oil in the engine. Too much end play will allow the crank to beat against the thrust bearing, eventually wearing or cracking it.

MIKING THE CRANK

Use a good quality micrometer to measure, or mike, the main journals. To get a good feel on the mike for tightening it down, use a ratchet mike. Several readings must be taken across each journal from left to right and all around the journal. This tells you if the journal is tapered or out-of-round. The difference between the room temperature and your hand's body temperature can change the mike setting by as much as .0002-inch. This must be considered an extreme accuracy error. So, the readings are taken on the journals from left to right (and recorded as each one is made), then they are rechecked in the same order again to minimize this inaccuracy. A crank which varies more than .0005-inch out-of-round should not be used for competition.

Check the photo of our notebook page showing the journal diameters we measured on the Moldex 350 crank we measured for our sample engine. The diameters did not vary more than .0002-inch.

Once the main bearing journals have been miked, repeat the same miking process on the rod journals.

The next thing to determine is the bearing clearances, so the main bearing sizes must be taken. To do this, the bearings must be inserted into the block and the caps torqued down. Use a good quality dial bore gauge (such as the Sunnen DK3280) to read the inside diameters of the bearing. Record these measurements in your notebook also. To determine the main bearing clearance, subtract the crankshaft main journal size from the main bearing size. The remainder is the main bearing clearance. The same procedure can be used to determine the rod bearing clearances.

Standard bearings can vary in thickness by .002 to .004-inch. If the spread between the bearings are within this range, different inserts can be juggled, in whole or halves, to find the clearances desired. And in case your crank has been ground undersize slightly, TRW offers its CL-77 main bearings .001 and .002-inch oversize.

A few tips about bearings: Always wipe the bearing off with lacquer thinner, front and back, to clean it before installing it (both in fitting and in final assembly). Also use lacquer thinner to clean the bore opening in which the bearing will set. When main bearing caps are torqued down, torque each bolt a little at a time, going back and forth from left to right. If the crankshaft end play is too small, decrease the thrust bearing side thickness with medium grit emery cloth.

OILING

For the type of extensive forces a crankshaft receives in any type of oval track or road racing, a cross-drilled crank is a must. Cross drilling assures a constant source of oil to all the journals through 360 degrees of crankshaft rotation. Without cross drilling, the crank receives oil pressure through only 180 degrees of rotation.

With a cross drilled crank, use a grooved bearing insert for the upper half of the bearing, and a solid bearing for the bottom half. The upper grooving assures more constant lubrication. The bottom half is not grooved because it needs as much surface area as possible to support the tremendous forces which are trying to push the crank out of the engine.

All of the oil hole openings onto the journals must be chamfered. This prevents rough openings from scraping grooves in the bearing surfaces. It also improves the flow of oil out of the crank to the bearings.

Some people will argue that cross drilling and grooved upper bearing halves can both be eliminated if the crank journals are grooved. This is an unwise practice. A crank groove is a good stress point for a crack to start. Further, Wilson points out, the smaller grooves weaken the strength of the crank considerably (the greatest strength of any tube-shaped surface is at its smallest O.D.).

CLEANING

Once all other procedures are carried out on the crankshaft, it should be ground with a small hand-held high-speed grinder inside all the oil passages to remove all possible sludge and flash. These are elements which could dislodge during operation, causing a ruined bearing and journal. Once this is done, use a drill-driven brush under a

[Reproduced from notebook page.]

CLEARANCES

MAINS

	1	2	3	4	5 (Thrust)
Bearings	2.4510	2.4511	2.4510	2.4512	2.4510
Journals	2.4482	2.4483	2.4481	2.4483	2.4482
Clearance	.0028	.0028	.0029	.0029	.0028

RODS

	1	2	3	4
Bearing	2.1013	2.1012	2.1015	2.1014
Journal	2.0987	2.0987	2.0988	2.0988
Clearance	.0026	.0025	.0027	.0026

	5	6	7	8
Bearing	2.1015	2.1015	2.1014	2.1013
Journal	2.0989	2.0989	2.0988	2.0988
Clearance	.0026	.0026	.0026	.0025

After all machining operations are completed on the crank, a stiff bristled brush powered by a drill is used with cleaning solvent to thoroughly clean all oil passages.

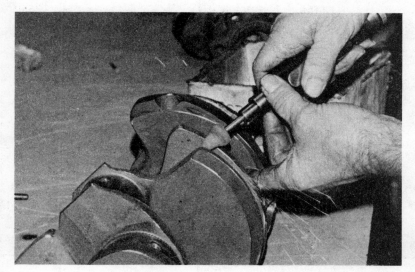

The crank counterweights must be thoroughly radiused.

Wilson checks the inside diameter of main bearings with dial bore gauge to determine clearance for crank. All main bearing caps should be torqued to proper specification and all main bearings should be checked at once.

stream of clean solvent to further clean out all the oil passages. Once the crank has been cleaned, use a small examination light to check all passages for any further debris.

RADIUSING

If the crank journals need to be ground smaller, the union of the flat journal surface to the cheeks of the throws must be carefully radiused. That is, a very smooth, round union must be shaped to do away with a sharp shoulder. The sharp joint will create stress lines which can grow and break the crank.

STROKING

Altering the stroke of a crankshaft means that other components must also be changed. If the stroke is increased and the same pistons and rods were retained, the longer stroke would push the piston out of the block (above the deck height). When the stroke is increased, the rod length must

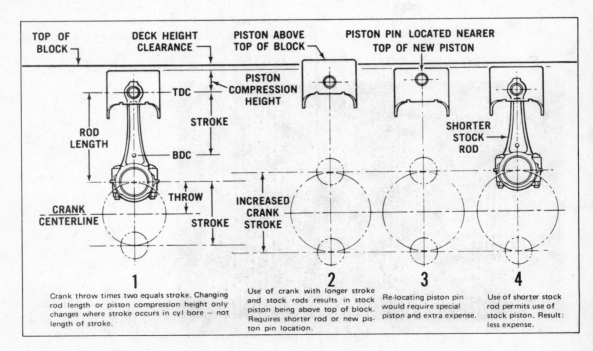

1 Crank throw times two equals stroke. Changing rod length or piston compression height only changes where stroke occurs in cyl bore — not length of stroke.

2 Use of crank with longer stroke and stock rods results in stock piston being above top of block. Requires shorter rod or new piston pin location.

3 Re-locating piston pin would require special piston and extra expense.

4 Use of shorter stock rod permits use of stock piston. Result: less expense.

be shortened by one-half the amount of the stroke increase. Or, if the same rods are retained, new pistons must be forged which have the wrist pin hole moved upward the distance of one-half the stroke increase. A decreased stroke would require a lengthened rod or a piston with the wrist pin hole lowered.

An increase in the stroke also means the piston will be compressing a greater volume, thus the piston dome or cylinder head chamber must be altered to keep the compression ratio the same. When ordering a set of pistons from a high performance component manufacturer, be sure to inform him of all these aspects, and he will make all the necessary changes in the piston.

Any time a stroker crank is installed in an engine, rotate it (with rods and pistons installed) fully through several revolutions to check for interference conditions. The most common interferences with strokers is counterweight-to-piston skirt and counterweight-to-block. Any interfering components must be notched.

TUFTRIDING

The "Tuftride" chemical heat treating process improves journal hardness and gives greater fatigue strength for high performance durability. Any crankshaft used in high performance competition should be Tuftrided.

Technically, the process is a chemical and metallurgical treatment of ferrous metal parts using a molten cyanide salt bath at a temperature of 1060 degrees F.

When carbon steels, such as crankshafts, are submerged in the bath, carbon and nitrogen are released, forming an iron carbide surface which greatly resists wear and lowers the coefficient of friction, while the nitrogen penetrates the metal making it tougher and more resistant to the formation of fatigue cracks.

As a result of the tough case of iron nitrides on the surface and the diffusion zone under it, wear resistance is increased 100% to 500%, fatigue strength is increased up to 88% and friction is reduced 40%. All this is accomplished without making the crankshaft brittle, which is the result of many other hardening processes.

INDEXING

Opposing crankshaft throws are designed to be spaced exactly 90 degrees apart. But, through the marvel of wide manufacturing tolerances, even the best of the passenger car cranks may not be spaced, or indexed, correctly.

The indexing process is one which a professional crankshaft service company can perform for you—and it is an important one. Let's assume your crank has the first throw ground .025-inch off to the right (or after top dead center). The two pistons operating from this throw would always be extended too far up into the bore as the plug fires. This makes the engine slightly out-of-time, causing a reduction in power output.

What is the answer to this dilemma? The answer largely depends on how great the error is. If it is slight, the crank can be offset ground .010-inch and oversize bearings can be used. It can also be welded and reground. If the error is too great, a

Crankshaft is mounted in dynamic balancing machine. First of bobweights is mounted on farthest left journal.

new crank would be a cheaper route to take.

BALANCING

To balance a crankshaft, first all reciprocating weights must be balanced. These include the pistons, pins, pin locks, rings, and small end of the rod. These items are staticly brought into balance with each other by weighing them and reducing all weight to that of the lightest.

Once the reciprocating weight is determined, it is duplicated about the crankshaft with bob weights. These simulate the reciprocating weights rotating about the crank. The bob weight is computed by adding 50% of the reciprocating weight to 100% of the rotating weight (which is the big end of the rod plus the bearings). The crank and weights are then spun in a balancing machine which automatically tells the operator where the crank is out of balance and by how much weight.

Balancing is an exacting and accurate procedure which should be performed on any engine slated for competition. A crankshaft out-of-balance puts a terrific strain on the main bearings and deflects with great force internally, creating stress cracks.

DAMPNER

Wilson recommends that all harmonic dampners be honed-out slightly for less interference fit so it is easier to slip them onto the crank. When installing the dampner, do not drive the dampner on but rather pull it on with a bolt. Driving it on will put stress against the thrust bearing, making it brittle.

The preferred Chevy small block dampner is part number 3817173—a 327 high performance heavy dampner.

With the Ford 351-C engine, use the Boss 302 dampner, part number C9ZZ 6316-B.

For the MoPar 340 engine, Chrysler recommends the use of the larger Hemi-engine dampner. The part number is P2532202. Because of the increased size of this dampner, a new front chain case cover, part number 3690714, is required.

For all racing engines, it is very convenient to use a degreed dampner. The dampner should be scribed at TDC and at every 90 degrees from TDC. A mark for total ignition advance (such as 38 degrees) should be scribed.

STRAIGHTENING

The maximum allowable runout (or bend) in the crankshaft is .001-inch. This is measured by setting the crankshaft in the block (with bearings), then measuring the crank along all the main journals with a dial indicator, while rotating the crank.

A crankshaft cannot be straightened in a hydraulic press without creating stress cracks. However, all of the major high performance crankshaft specialty companies can straighten cranks with a hammering process.

After checking the straightness, bolt on the end and center main bearing caps. Then check the deck readings (as we describe in detail in the block chapter of this book).

POLISHING

The last operation on the crankshaft before its installation is polishing the journals. The purpose of polishing is to smooth out any tiny nicks which could scratch the bearing surface.

An absolutely smooth finish is not desired. The metal has to have a somewhat rough surface so the oil has some pores in the metal in which to cling.

To polish the crank, use a #400 grit Carborendum belt. Always break in a new polishing belt on the throws to avoid accidentally putting a groove in the journals. As the polishing belt is applied with a light touch over the journals, be sure not to let it taper the journals or get them out-of-round.

As a final step, run emery cloth over the rear main oil seal journal. Any nicks on this surface

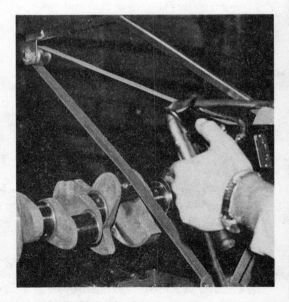

The crank journals are polished very carefully with a light pressure. Care must be taken so journal shape is not distorted.

Engine	Part #	Material	Stroke	Rod Journal Dia.	Main Bearing Dia.
Chevrolet 350	3941184	Forged Steel	3.480	2.100	2.4508
Chevrolet 350	3997748	Forged steel	*	*	*
MoPar 340	2843868	Forged Steel	3.310	2.125	2.500
MoPar 355	MOLDEX	Forged Steel	3.461	2.125	2.500
Ford 351-C	D1ZZ-6303-A	Modular Iron	3.500	2.311	2.749
Ford 351-C	MOLDEX	Forged Steel	*	*	*

* These cranks can be finished to your specifications.

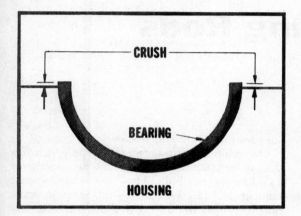

Bearing material excess which extends above bearing cap is known as its crush. When the cap is torqued down the bearing insert is forced to conform with bore.

After balancing, the crank should be cleaned with solvent as we described. Then wipe the journals with lacquer thinner and mike the crank for bearing clearances. Polishing is the last operation after miking, because good micrometers (which have carbide tips) could very possibly nick the journals. Polishing will erase these small nicks.

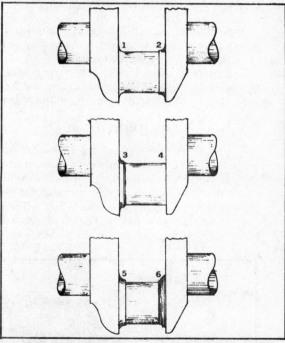

Six different journal fillets are illustrated here with only #1 being correct. It is very round and smooth to form a gentle transition from the journal to the counter-weight or cheek. Number 2 is a round stepped fillet. Cracks will develop at the step. Number 3 has a partial radius, but it is still too rough. Number 4 has zero radius and will develop stress cracks the quickest. Number 5 is a reground crank where the fillet did not blend into the journal. Number 6 is a rough transition, generally the way stock crank shafts are delivered from the factory.

could tear up the rear main seal. This journal cannot be too smooth, however, because the neoprene seal will stick to it if it is.

DO IT RIGHT

If you suspect the crankshaft to be inaccurate in either journal size or indexing, check it to be sure before you do anything else. There is no use in balancing, deburring, polishing and cleaning, and **then** discovering that one journal is inaccurate.

Taking things in a logical order of sequence, anything pertaining to the machining of the crank (even rough deburring) should be done before balancing. Any metal removal from the crank after balancing will affect the balance of it.

Connecting Rods

The connecting rod, being it is subjected to such punishing circumstances, can possibly be the most volatile part of the racing engine.

Care must be taken in selecting, sizing, Magnafluxing, grinding and shotpeening any rod being used in order to insure its longevity in the engine.

WHICH ROD TO USE

We'll examine the case of the Chevrolet small block first. Through the early development of the 350 for NASCAR Grand National racing, Wilson found that an adequate factory part did not exist, so he relied heavily on those made by Carillo and CSC (Crank Shaft Company). They both proved to be excellent rods, existing in many 500-mile super-

speedway races with no problems.

Chevrolet has introduced a new rod which fills the gap for small block racing. The part number is 343710. The rod bolt which goes with it is part number 343713. This bolt is the knurled shank boron steel 7/16" bolt which proved to be extremely durable in the big block LS-6 engines, but it is not interchangeable with the big block rod bolt as the small block bolt is .020" shorter. This 343710 rod will come to you from the Chevy dealer in an unfinished form, with the wrist pit hole undrilled. A Bridgeport mill will be required to drill it. Bill Howell at Chevrolet tells us the rod material itself will not be difficult to drill. The reason for Chevrolet selling the rod this way is

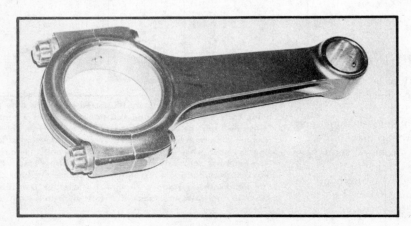

The H-beam construction of this Carillo rod makes it mighty strong. Notice how shoulder of rod and bearing have been radiused for clearance on the crank journal radius.

the versatility it provides. The center-to-center length can be anywhere from 5.7" to 6.150", depending on how you drill the hole. After the hole is drilled, it must be deburred, and then shotpeened. Part number 366232 is the finished version of the 343710 rod (6.0" length).

Ford has a high strength rod available for the 351-C which they call "the highest strength, highest quality rod ever produced by Ford." It is forged from 1041 fine grain steel and is shotpeened and Magnafluxed at the factory. However the rods should be ground and polished, so shotpeening must be performed again on them.

The part number is M-6200-A351. The rod bolts are part number D1ZZ 6214-A, and the nuts are part number D1ZZ 6212-A. The bolts are 3/8-inch diameter, heat-treated to a tensile strength of 180,000 psi.

These are not the rods which Wilson uses for Grand National Ford engines, although they would be a good choice for a small track motor. Wilson rcommends the Crower rods for the best durability in a big-track engine. Carillo rods are also available for the 351-C.

Chrysler Corporation has introduced an excellent rod for the 340 which has proven itself already in 500-mile superspeedway events. It is part number P3614514. Use rod bolt and nut set number P4120070 (7/16" dia.). These rods come from the factory already polished and shotpeened, but it is still a good idea to at least have them Magnafluxed. The rod bolts are high quality 7/16" diameter. The rod itself is modeled after the very durable 426 Hemi engine rods.

Another special forged steel racing rod which Chrysler has made available for oval track racing is part number P3690641. It can use the same rod

bolts and nuts as previously mentioned. This rod is entirely adequate for all short track racing.

PREPARING RODS

All production rods which come from the factories have a forging parting seam along the beam which needs to be ground off. In addition, all sharp edges should be rounded. The grinding should be done lengthwise on the rod, and ground very smooth. After finish grinding, it should be polished with a belt of #400 grit. A high-speed hand grinder should also be used to round all sharp edges around the rod bolt head and nut seats, and to smooth any nicks in the radius of the bolt and nut seats. After grinding and polishing, all rods should be Magnaflux inspected, along with the bolts and nuts. A final step would be shotpeening, which builds in a very high surface compressive strength on the rod (don't shotpeen the bolts and nuts). The Chevrolet factory specifications for shotpeening are: .012-.015". Allmen "A" Arc height using #230 cast steel shot.

As a further step of insurance, it is a good idea to have the rods and especially the bolts hardness tested on a Rockwell tester. A typical forged steel rod should have a 27-34 Rockwell hardness on the C scale, and a bolt should have a 36-40 Rockwell "C" hardness.

PIN OILING

The small end of the rod must be reworked for wrist pin oiling. To do this, drill a 1/8" hole through the top of the rod all the way to the wrist pin bore. Counterbore the top of the hole with a

In the photo at left, the edge of the rod bearing insert is straight and square. At the right, the bearing insert has been radiused to clear the radiused fillet of the crank. If this isn't done, the square edge of the bearing will wear a stress point into the radius. Also, you won't have the proper side clearance if the radius isn't cut on the bearings.

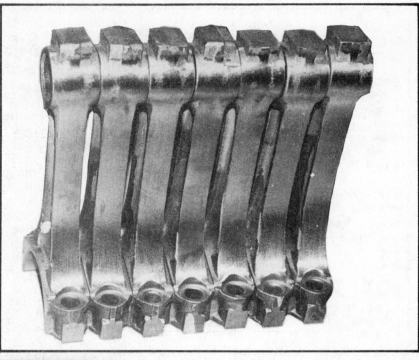

Chevy rods which have been ground and polished.

Chevy rod has to have sides ground and polished to remove forging parting seam. Rod is shot-peened after grinding.

A Sunnen rod honing machine is used to size and index rods.

This is the proper way to drill a pin oiling hole in the top of a rod. Counterbored hole funnels oil into bearing.

Side view drawing shows how oil is funneled to pin by top-drilled hole.

#4 or #5 center drill to a depth of 1/4'', so the cavity will act as a funnel to feed the oil into the pin.

This process is a controversial one, as many people say the best method of wrist pin oiling is to drill two holes up from the bottom end of the rod. Wilson, Junior Johnson and many other Grand National engine builders have tried this method and have reverted back to the single hole at the top. The reason for using the single top hole is better oil supply creating less wrist pin galling.

Wilson tried a Chevy 427 LS rod in a 350 small block. The extra rod length forced the wrist pin hole up beyond the oil control ring. Buttons had to be used as pin retainers. The two holes on the bottom of the pin boss on each side were drilled by the piston maker, which is a mistake. These holes serve to severely weaken the strength of the piston.

SIZING

To be sure that all rod bores are parallel and round and the center-to-center lengths are the same on all the rods, they should be sized and reworked in a Sunnen rod reconditioning machine.

The method of sizing Wilson recommends is to first slightly sand the parting surfaces of the cap and rod on an 8'' x 10'' piece of sandpaper taped to any **flat** surface. This assures they are straight and parallel and will have no binding force on one side of the bearing insert. It also removes any nicks or burrs on the rod or cap which could cause them to be ground imperfectly. Then a slight amount of material is removed from the mating surfaces on the Sunnen rod and cap grinder. The rod and cap are cleaned and torqued together with bolts oiled to the required specs for that particular rod and bolt. Because the mating surfaces have been

Side clearance between the pair of rods is held in place with feeler gauge strips while rod bolts are torqued.

ground, the rod bore is smaller, so it is then honed in the Sunnen rod honing machine, and carefully checked with a dial bore gauge.

SIDE CLEARANCE

The maximum side clearance allowable between any pair of rods is .018" to .022". Any more than this will cause the rod to "snake" or wobble. Too little clearance will not let the hot oil flow out properly, which could cause bearing failure.

If the side clearance needs to be enlarged by just a small amount, the rods can be polished on a flat plate using #180 grit paper. Otherwise, a large amount of material must be removed on a surface grinder.

ALUMINUM RODS

When it comes to this subject, we like to quote Ralph Moody, who said: "I'd be scared to use an aluminum rod for a quarter-mile trophy dash."

Aluminum rods may have their place in drag racing, but definitely not in oval track and road racing. Aluminum has a much less strength-to-density ratio than forged steel, so for the same load bearing strength an aluminum rod must have much more material to it, cancelling out any

weight savings.

The only good these rods serve in drag racing engines is to serve as a shock absorber (because they are flexible) in situations where high detonation is prevalent.

ROD-TO-STROKE RATIO

Connecting rods which are long in relation to a given stroke will tend to peak the engine's torque at a higher RPM range. A short rod-to-stroke ratio will make an engine's torque peak at a lower RPM. Most common rod-to-stroke ratios range between 1.6 to 1 and 1.9 to 1. A good mid-range torque engine will have approximately a 1.7 to 1 ratio. Wilson's recommendations for the Chevy 350 engine would be a 5.7-inch rod for a short track engine and a 6.0-inch rod for superspeedway application.

The ratio is determined by dividing the center-to-center rod length by the stroke. Long rods or short strokes (which yield lower ratios) create a faster piston velocity as the piston approaches

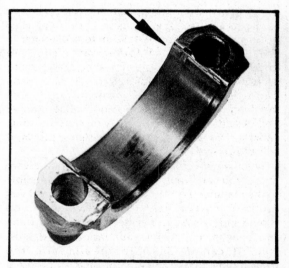

Notice the shoulder-step type of wear pattern on this rod bearing [see arrow]. This is a normal pattern indicating good bearing crush. This bearing has 600 miles of superspeedway racing on it.

TDC and BDC. This fact allows some leeway when the valves open and close in relationship to where the piston is. The slower this piston velocity is as it approaches TDC and BDC, the more critical the exact valve timing is.

Pistons

The first thing you will want to do when preparing to build a racing engine is to order your pistons. These components seem to take longer to arrive than almost any other part. They are important to have because almost no preparations can be made for building until the pistons are on hand. If you order your pistons from a large manufacturer and they are a standard part number and design, the time element won't be too long. However, if you order a custom designed piston, it will take longer.

When ordering pistons, it will be to your advantage if you can supply all the information possible to the manufacturer to insure the ones you get will do the job you expect. The information you should supply should include: engine type, bore, stroke, head cc's, compression ratio desired, gross cam lift, cam duration, rocker arm ratio, rod length, type, brand and size of rings to be used, and pressed or full-floating pin.

WHICH KIND OF PISTONS

The first thing to consider is forged pistons. Forged aluminum pistons are the only type which should be used for all-out high performance. It is difficult to control thermal expansion with stock-type cast pistons in a racing condition. Further, high temperature structural strength is also lacking in cast pistons. TRW claims that forged pistons offer much greater strength without added

weight, they run cooler and dissipate heat more quickly.

There exists a multitude of piston manufacturers and piston designs. When considering which ones to purchase, consider these elements which set good pistons apart from mediocre ones: structural strength, heat dissipation, distortion

Using a fine grit sandpaper cone, commonly called pencil rolls, on a high speed grinder, all sharp edges on piston are radiused. Notice how piston is carefully secured to guard against nicks. Don't clamp a piston in a vise!

under high cylinder pressure, and horsepower loss due to friction. We have listed below pistons by brand and part number for particular applications because these pistons have been found to be superior in these departments:

Engine	Mfgr. & Part #	Compression
Chevy 350	TRW L2252AF	12.5 to 1
Ford 351	Venolia 483NA	Specify
MoPar 340	MoPar P3690848 and 849	12.0 to 1

COMPRESSION RATIO

All pistons for engines we are concentrating on in this book (Chevy 350, MoPar 340 and Ford 351-C) use domed tops to attain a 12.0 or 12.5 to 1 compression ratio. Each one of these engines, also, has more than one design of cylinder head chamber. When you receive your pistons, be sure the dome mates to the head chamber design you are employing. Also, be sure to check the compression ratio (how to do this is covered in a separate chapter).

Piston dome size and shape has as much to do with compression ratio as cylinder head volume. Keep this in mind if you bore the cylinders oversize. With the larger bore, the piston is compressing more volume, so the compression ratio will go up. To remedy this, either head chamber volume must be increased or the piston dome shape must be changed. Some piston

Note: Diamond Racing has a small block Chevy forged piston available. The basic forging is by TRW.

manufacturers—TRW for one—automatically decrease the dome size to compensate for an oversize bore.

CLEARANCES

The first thing to do when you get your pistons and block is to mate the pistons to the cylinders and check them for clearances. Measure the bore with a dial bore gauge or snap gauge and micrometer. Measure the piston with a micrometer at the wrist pin centerline, 90 degrees from the pin opening. This is done because this is the rocking point of the piston. Once clearances for each piston and bore are found, mark the piston with the cylinder number for which it was mated in a manner which will not come off the piston. You will find that the pistons vary in size slightly, so the finished hone of each cylinder will vary slightly in order to accomplish a uniform desired clearance in all cylinders.

Proper piston-to-cylinder wall clearance is vitally important. Too much clearance will cause the piston to rock in the bore, causing cylinder wall scratches and abnormal wear. It will also lead to poor ring sealing, allowing blow-by. Piston rocking over a prolonged period can also lead to cylinder wall cracking. Too little clearance can cause piston and/or cylinder wall galling.

A TRW Chevy 350 piston right out of the box. Notice all the sharp edges on the top. These must be radiused to prevent hot spots.

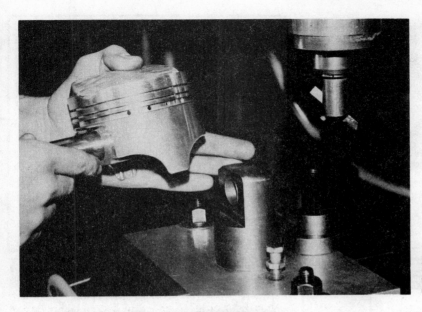

The piston is fitted on a special jig for machining of the piston flat surfaces. The piston is located with its pin to maintain accuracy among all pistons.

The Bridgeport mill takes a .010 in. cut off flat of piston. Lubrication oil is sprayed at piston while being milled to prevent galling.

The piston clearances Wilson has found to be best are as follows:

1) Piston to bore: .0065 to .007"
2) Ring end gap: .017" on top ring and .015" on second ring
3) Wrist pin: .008". This is for a full-floating pin and encompasses both piston pin-to-rod and piston pin-to-piston clearances
4) Wrist pin end play: .000" to .005. The less the better to preserve the locks.

MACHINING

Although the pistons we have specified by make and part number come from the manufacturer in good, ready-to-use condition, a few machining operations to them are vital to increase engine longevity, reduce friction, insure uniformity and increase horsepower.

All of the machining operations we discuss in this section should be performed by a competant machine shop, such as Waddell Wilson's, which is familiar with these operations and has fixtures available to hold the pistons properly while these operations are carried out.

The first machining operation is to true-up the piston, locating it with the pin centerline to assure that the distance from pin hole centerline to piston top is uniform. The piston is put in a fixture which locates it in the pin hole, and is trued in a Bridgport mill. Once the piston is in the fixture, a dial indicatior is used to measure the bottom ring land on each side of the piston. This is done to be sure it is setting in the fixture in a position which would be perpendicular to the cylinder walls. Then .010" is taken off the flat quench area of the piston top. This assures that all the pistons are uniform before the deck measurement is taken.

After this operation, the Bridgeport mill is used to machine fire slots through the piston domes, angled toward the exhaust valve. This slot has proven to gain about 8 horsepower because of better flame travel.

Because the top surface of the piston is the hottest, it expands more than the rest of the piston

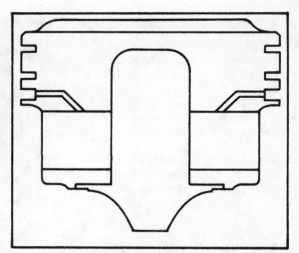

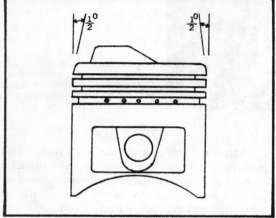

Top, the top ring land is tapered on a lathe. Drawing illustrates how piston is tapered.

Above, the Bridgeport mill is used to drill angled pin oiling hole in piston. The cutaway piston view at top shows where pin oiling holes are drilled.

In upper pin boss, notice oiling hole which is angled from oil ring groove. Also notice how complete interior of piston has been deburred, sanded and radiused to eliminate any stress points. In the bottom pin hole, it can be seen how the piston was machined for double spirolox retainers.

from the top surface down to the top of the first ring groove. To combat this, the piston is tapered in this area 1½ degrees to reduce the drag on the cylinder wall.

TRW pistons are machined for a .038" thick pin lock. Wilson desires to use the much stronger .072" Spirolox pin retainers, so the groove in the piston has to be widened .034" outward for the thicker locks.

A modification which improves pin oiling and thus pin durability is an oil slot which is drilled from the oil ring groove to intersect with another slot drilled up at an angle from the piston pin hole. This hole must be drilled directly above the centerline of the piston pin hole.

Instead of drilling this angle oil slot, many people think they can improve pin oiling by drilling holes up from the bottom of the piston pin bosses. This is a tragic mistake. The pin bosses receive the highest loading stresses of the piston, thus holes in this area weaken the piston considerably.

The last preparatory operation to be performed on any set of pistons is to completely deburr and round-off all sharp edges on the piston. This operation should be done with a hand-held high speed grinder. Sharp edges and burrs on the piston can cause hot spots which could cause preignition.

FLYCUTTING

Sometimes high cam lift makes it necessary to flycut pistons, or notch the piston top for increased valve clearance. Flycutting tools can be purchased or rented from several of the leading camshaft manufacturers. When the flycutting procedure is being done, be careful to take out only the minimum amount of material necessary. Piston dome thickness must never be less than .200". Anything less will seriously weaken the piston.

PISTON GALLING

Galled pistons and walls have several causes, all of which can be avoided with some attention to detail. The most frequent causes are: (1) washing the cylinder walls down with gasoline (carburetor needle and seat are bad, or plug is fouled); (2) improper piston-to-wall clearance (too tight a clearance); (3) warming the engine up improperly (the combustion chamber is hot right away, so the piston expands immediately, but the cylinder wall is still surrounded by cold water, so it doesn't grow. The best warm-up procedure is to hold the RPMs at 2000 until the water temperature is at 180 degrees.)

WRIST PINS

There are two types of wrist pins available—pressed-in and full-floating. Chevrolet and Chrysler both recommend the full-floating design. Ford goes with the pressed-in pin.

Through years of racing engine preparation, Wilson has formed the opinion that full floating pins are the best application for high performance engines. There are two reasons: first, because racing engines are assembled and disassembled quite often, it makes assembly easier. Second, lubrication for a pressed-in pin can be marginal, allowing excessive wear and eventual failure.

The argument against full-floating pins is that the rod "snakes" around on the pin. This won't happen if the rod side clearances are correct—no more than .018" to .022" side clearance.

The TRW and MoPar pistons specified earlier in the chapter come set-up for full floating pins. The Venolia pistons need only to be specified to be set-up for full-floating pins.

Pin end clearance is very important with full-floating pins. Anywhere from .000 to .005" is recommended, the less the better to keep the locks intact. If the end clearance exceeds the recommendations, the pin will act as a battering ram and knock the pins out.

To help retention of the pins, Wilson recommends the use of .072" thick Spiralox pin locks. Of the three types commonly used in racing applications, he has found these to give the best performance. Once an engine is torn down and the pin locks are removed, throw them away and use new ones for reassembly. It's cheap insurance.

A new development in piston pins is the lightweight tapered wall pin. It is available from Venolia and Diamond for any piston. Its strength lies in the fact that the greater part of the stresses encountered by the pin are concentrated in a thicker cross-sectional area, yet the pin still does not add that much weight to the total assembly.

PISTON RINGS

Finding the correct piston ring combination which provides cylinder sealing, good oil control and little friction is the key to unleashing more potential horsepower.

The rings recommended by Wilson are the Speed-Pro brand manufactured by the Sealed Power Corp. They are especially made for high performance applications.

The top two compression rings should be no thicker than 1/16" to reduce frictional drag area, and to avoid the possibility of ring flutter. Flutter is an inward deflection of the ring caused by high inertia placed on it during the power stroke. As the width is decreased, the inertia is decreased.

A 3/16" thick oil ring is preferred. It does a better job of controlling the oil, at no cost of horsepower. In addition, using a taller oil ring also allows the oil return holes in the ring groove to be larger, making the return easier and oil build-up frictional drag less.

It is recommended that the top two rings be moly coated. The face of the rings in these is filled with porous molybdenum to give the ultimate in lubrication. Oil embeds in the porosity of the moly coating, acting as a lube reservoir to help reduce wear on the cylinder walls. Molybdenum has a lower coefficient of friction than chrome or cast iron (the two other ring materials), yet has a much greater hardness and higher melting point, so the moly ring has a much greater resistance to scuffing. A side benefit of moly rings is that they provide quick seating.

Chrome-plated rings should be considered, however, if the engine is going to be used in an extremely dusty condition. Chrome is more resistant to abrasive wear.

The top compression ring should not extend into the groove at a depth any greater than .005". If it goes in any deeper, compression loss can result. If the ring does go in deeper, use a TRW spacer #TSR431C.

RING END GAP

When checking the ring end gap, put the ring into the cylinder and use some type of cylinder (such as a coffee can) to squarely push the ring into the bore. (Be sure to fit the rings to the bores **after** the cylinders have been honed.) If the ring is placed in the bore slightly cocked, a faulty end

gap results.

Use a feeler gauge to determine what the existing end gap is. If the gap must be increased, it must be properly filed. Place a file in a vise and move the ring against it from the outside diameter of the ring to the inside diameter. Never file in the opposite direction, because this will cause the surface which seals against the cylinder walls to

Any flat bottomed cylinder can be used to push piston rings squarely into bores. Notice rings in first two bores. This is proper method for checking ring end gap. Rings must not be cocked in bores, or a faulty end gap reading will result.

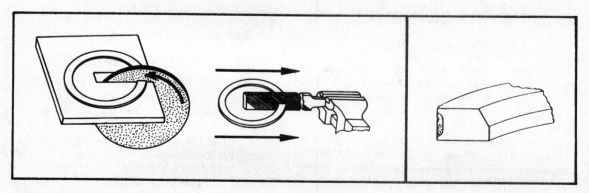

Left, when increasing ring end gap, ring should only be filed in one direction to prevent outside edge of ring from being chipped. At right, drawing shows how moly material is imbedded into a ring.

chip or crack. Once the desired end gap has been achieved, break the sharp edges of the ring ends with a 400 grit emery cloth.

Be sure the end gap does not exceed the recommended specification. If it does, blow-by will result, causing a power loss, fouled plugs and preignition. Compression loss will also result. Too little end gap will let the ring butt together which damages the ring. If the ring ends are shiny when they are removed from an engine which has been run, the gap has closed and the ends have rubbed together.

GAP PLACEMENT

End gap placement in relationship to the other ring ends is important so the gaps will not line up and provide a direct access for blow-by. The oil expander ring gap should be directly above the centerline of the wristpin hole in the piston. The top oil rail gap should be one inch to the left of

the expander's gap, and the bottom oil rail gap should be one inch to the right of the expander gap.

The second compression ring gap should be one inch to the left of the top oil rail gap, and the top compression ring gap should be one inch to the right of the bottom oil rail gap.

BALANCING

Balancing of all reciprocating parts, such as the piston, pin and rod assemblies, is a critical operation which leads to more power output (reciprocating vibrations eat up horsepower). This operation should be carried out by an experienced expert in this field, such as Waddell Wilson's. Once all assemblies have been balanced, keep a record of the weight of each component so that replacement of one piston, one pin or one rod does not require rebalancing of the entire assembly.

35 P cu in   *Stroke 3⁷⁄₆ minus .0025*

Name _Darrell Waltrip_   Date _____   Eng. #_____

Address _____   Date Promised _____

TRW pistons # L22527   REMARKS _new block_

Carillo rods

	Wt.(grams)	Size		
			525	Rotating end of (1) Conn Rod
			525	Rotating end of (1) Conn Rod
Piston	690	___	91	Bearing Inserts or Insert
Piston Pin	___	___	6	Oil
Piston Rings	42	___	736	(1) Piston
Pin Locks	4	___		(1) Piston Pin
Total Rod	703	___		(1) Set Piston Rings
Recip. Rod	178	___		(1) Set Pin Locks
Rot. Rod	525	___	178	Reciprocating End of (1)
Insert	91	___		Conn. Rod
			2061	Total Weight of (1) Bob Weight
	1030½			

(28.35 Grams = 1 ounce)

Wilson prepares and keeps on file a card like this one for each engine he builds which records balance weight of all components in it.

Cylinder Block Preparation

The cylinder block is going to be the home for everything else contained in and on the engine, so good engine preparation starts here. If all tolerances are exact on the block, and all block dimensions are true, then you are on your way to a precision engine assembly.

WHICH BLOCK TO USE

If you are purchasing a new block, use the following part numbers: (1) Chevrolet 350, #366246 (This is a bare block with four-bolt main caps); (2) Ford 351-C, #M-6015-A3, and (3) Chrysler 340, #P3690898.

If you can locate one of these blocks in a used car or wrecking yard, you will be money ahead. Further, a used block, providing it is not excessively worn or is not cracked, is more desirable. New blocks, no matter how good the quality, generally shift about slightly during the beginning of their life from the stresses of warming up and cooling off. A used block, you can be assured, has settled all it's going to, and your precision machining will not be wasted.

If you get a used block, the first step is to take out all the freeze plugs and oil galley plugs, and have it hot tanked. Then any block, new or used,

should be visually inspected for flaws and cracks, then Magnaflux inspected for cracking.

The first order of business in block blueprinting is to thoroughly grind off all casting flash and burrs on the block. These unwanted bits of material can work loose and find their way into the lubrication system. In new blocks, small pockets of sand from casting can always be found in hidden corners. The entire block inner surface should be ground smooth and polished with a hand grinder to remove any rough surface which can impede the flow of oil back to the pan. The grinder is also used to radius all sharp edges. Be extremely careful when deburring and polishing the block with a hand grinder. One slip into the tappet bores, cylinder bores or across a gasket sealing surface can ruin everything.

The tappet bores must be honed out with a wheel cylinder hone to clean any burrs off and give a good cross hatch pattern on which an oil film clings to lubricate the tappets. Be careful not to hone these bores too much—the desired tappet clearance is .0015-.0025-inch.

The block's drive-in freeze plugs are anchored by three small Allen-head screws each. Drill the holes 3/16" deep with a number 35 drill, then tap it for threads. There is a danger of drilling into the

Key Dimensions

A Bore
B Stroke
C Bore Spacing
D Crankshaft Main
   Journal Dia.
E Crankshaft Rod
   Journal Dia.
F Cam Journal Dia.
G ℄ of Crank to Top of
   Block (Head Face)

H Block Deck
   Height Clearance
I Piston Compression
   Height
J Con Rod center-to-
   center length
K Intake and Exhaust
   Valve Head Dia.
L Valve Spring
   Installed Height

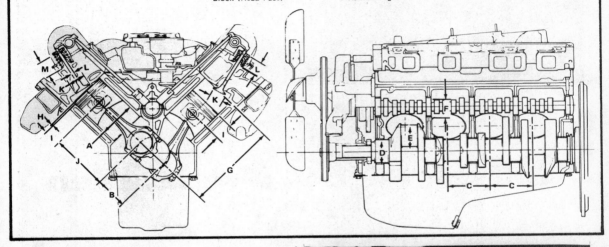

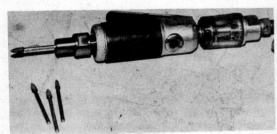

A high speed grinder and abrasive cones used for radiusing and polishing. These are the stones used for deburring and cleaning oil passages.

Above, a high speed grinder is used to clean the burrs and roughness from inside all oil galleys.

Left, The three Allen head pipe plugs replace knock-in plugs which are furnished with the block. The screw-in plugs assure they won't blow out. Be sure that the cam bearing oil inlet holes are lined up with the oil feed galleys in the block.

Even when a block has been torn down and is being rebuilt, all the threads are chased with a tap. Squeeze bottle at right holds light weight oil which is used to lube tap.

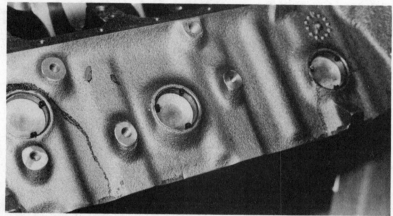

The Allen head screws securely locate the block freeze plugs. Everything is coated with Loctite to prevent leaks.

water jacket, so coat screws with Loctite.

All drive-in oil plugs must be knocked out and threaded for pipe plugs. When the plugs are installed, they should be lightly coated with Loctite. Before the plugs are put in place for final assembly of the block, an inspection light should be used to check all oil galleys for the least little bit of debris left in them. Don't leave anything to chance.

Cam bearings, whether you have a new block or an old one, should be driven out, the journals thoroughly cleaned, and new ones installed. Be sure to use the proper tool to drive the bearing out.

After the grinding operation, all threaded holes on the block should be oiled and chased with a tap. On both new and used blocks, you will find a variety of debris inhabiting these threads. Then the top of all the threaded holes, especially all the head stud holes, should be chamfered so the block material (from the first thread) will not pull up when the heads are torqued down.

Once these preparatory items are taken care of, the actual machining operations can begin. The first step is the lineboring, or align-honing. Align honing, with a Sunnen machine which is used by Waddell Wilson's, is preferred to align boring because the hone is less likely to move the crankshaft axis centerline upward toward the camshaft centerline. If this happens, the timing chain will be slack, creating timing inaccuracies. Special shorter chains are available from Cloyes if this has happened to your block. This is always a problem in align-honing, and thus only an experienced machine operator and shop should be entrusted to perform this work on your block.

For the operation of an engine on the street or occasional drag racing, etc., it might be allowable to fit the crank in the engine, torque down the main bearing caps, and see if the crank turns freely with no bind. But for a precision competition engine, the align-honing operation is a must. All main bearing caps and webs must be in perfect alignment and size, or a spun bearing or ruined crankshaft could result. Align-honing assures that all bearings are carrying the same load.

Before the block is align-honed, all main cap faces are ground flat and all cap mating faces are

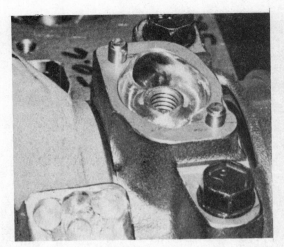

Notice how the oil pump boss in the rear main cap has been radiused and smoothed. The purpose is so that burrs and rough casting do not restrict the oil flow.

The deck/bore edges are radiused with fine grit sandpaper.

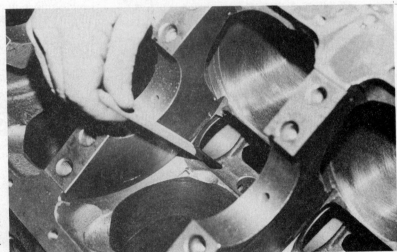

The file points to a sand pit left in a new block from casting. This has to be removed by grinding the block surface smooth.

A completely deburred block. You can run your hand all over it without feeling any sharp or rough places.

filed smooth and flat. Approximately .002-.003-inch of material is taken off. Then the main caps are bolted and torqued to specification and the block is inserted into the machine. Several cuts are taken, each in small increments, and a dial bore gauge is used to take measurements in between each cut. The final bore tolerances, in the main bearing saddles, as measured with the dial bore gauge, should be:

Chevrolet 350	2.6406"-2.6415"
Chrysler 340	2.6925"-2.6930"
Ford 351C	2.9417"-2.9425"

After align-honing, a trial fit of all the pistons and rods with crank and block is made to determine the deck height (the distance from the piston flat surface to the block deck, be it above or below the deck). At the same time this is being done, the deck is checked to see if it is parallel to the crankshaft axis centerline and perpendicular to the cylinder bores.

To make this check, the dial indicator base is anchored magnetically on the deck and the indicator measures how far down into the bore the piston flat is at TDC. The dial indicator should be positioned on top of the piston on the flat surface right above the piston pin on each side. This assures you won't get an error from the piston being cocked in the bore. To understand an actual situation, let's assume on a Chevy 350 engine we find along the left bank that the distance from the deck to the piston flat is, in order, .007", .009", .011" and .013". This shows the deck is tapered .006" from one end to the other in comparison to the crankshaft centerline. The deck will have to be milled to the height of the smallest clearance (.007"), so a cut of .0065" is taken off the deck in the milling machine. This leaves the deck-to-piston flat clearance (or deck height measurement) at .0065" on all four cylinders. Will this be enough clearance? The minimum distance from the piston flat to the cylinder head quench area must be .040". The compressed gasket thickness

of the two Chevy head gaskets we are using is .034" (.017" each), and the deck height clearance is .0065" below the deck, so .0065" and .034" add up to .0405", or .0005" over the minimum clearance.

To make the trial fit, the crankshaft, rods and pistons must first be completely prepared. All rods in the set must have been sized so they are the exact same length from center to center. Likewise, all pistons have to be sized and machined (as we described in the piston chapter elsewhere in this book). This makes all piston/rod assemblies the same length, so if the deck height check shows a variation among cylinders on the same bank, we know that the problem is block taper.

The metal finish left on the deck by the milling machine is good. A mirror-like finish is not desired on the deck or head because the head gasket needs some "tooth" to bite into. We have seen many head gasket failures result from a polished deck surface. After the block has been milled, the head stud holes must again be chamfered and tapped.

The next operation is the cylinder honing. Before this can be done, the piston-to-cylinder wall clearances must first be established. The desired

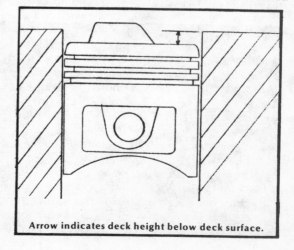

Arrow indicates deck height below deck surface.

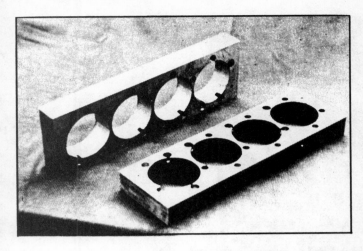

Cylinder block honing plates are shown at left. These plates should always be used to prevent cylinder distortion when honing the cylinder.

clearance is .007". To do this, each piston is mated to a cylinder, and the pistons are numbered according to their cylinder position. This is done because in a set of pistons, there is certain to be a variation among them as to actual diameter. That means in order to establish a uniform clearance in each cylinder, each bore must be honed to a different size to correspond to the piston. The piston diameter should be taken with a high-quality micrometer on a line exactly 90 degrees from the pin centerline. This measurement should be recorded right on the piston with a felt tip marking pen. The clearance of .007" is added to this diameter and this figure is recorded on the block by each bore with the marking pen. This is the size to which the cylinder will be honed.

Waddell Wilson uses the finest cylinder honing machine around, the Sunnen CK-10 Honemaster. This machine takes all the variables out of honing, such as coolant and lubricant feed, speed of the hone as it is pulled up and down, the cross-hatch pattern, etc. All of this is taken care of automatically. Wilson feels so strongly about the quality of this machine that he says a racer should haul his block to any lengths required in order to have it honed on one of these. Wilson also uses this machine to bring any oversize bore to size, even if the block is being overbored by .060". A rough grit stone is used to do the preliminary sizing to within .0025" of the desired finish, then finish stones are used for the final honing.

Before the honing is done, a couple of things should be done to the block first. The main caps should be installed and torqued to specification. The block will twist and distort as pressures from bolt torquing begin to set up internal stresses in it. This is because the block is a complex design of thick and thin sections which distort at different

rates. Likewise, a deck torquing plate should be used. The top of the cylinder block is affected by the torquing of the cylinder heads. If the deck plates are not used, the cylinders can certainly be finished to specifications and the bores found to be straight and round. But after the cylinder heads are torqued in place, things change. Instead of perfectly round bores, they are now distorted and irregular in shape. To counteract these additional mechanical stresses, it is necessary to prestress the top of the block, just as the lower end of it is stressed. This is accomplished with the deck plate. The plates are usually made from 2-inch or 3-inch thick steel. When selecting bolts for the deck plate, be sure they extend the same distance into the cylinder block as the regular head bolts. If the deck plate bolts are too long, they will go deeper into the unused portion of the tapped threads in the block and result in permanent cylinder distortion. The purpose of the deck plate would be entirely defeated if the improper length bolts were used. Also, when installing the deck plate, it is a good idea to use a head gasket of the type which will be used in the finished assembly.

This all might sound like a lot of trouble to go through for honing, but the results will be more perfect cylinder bores. Cylinders which are round and free of distortion allow the rings to seat quickly. Near perfect roundness at the top of the cylinder bore is extremely critical for all types of compression rings.

For the finish honing, Wilson uses a number 625 stone if chrome rings are going to be installed, and a number 820 stone if moly rings are to be used. Moly rings need a smoother finish. Use a slow stroke and fast speed on the CK-10 to get as smooth a finish as possible.

While the deck plate is still torqued onto the

Notice the cracked cylinder on this 340 block. It can be repaired by sleeving the cylinder. TRW makes the cylinder sleeves.

block, it is a good time to fit the rings for end gap. Remember that once the bolts are untorqued from the plate and block, the cylinders will again be distorted. After the ring end gap has been established for each ring in each cylinder, the ring should immediately be fitted to the piston for that cylinder.

After the deck plate is removed, the cylinder bore top edges should be radiused, smoothed and polished.

Before the block is used for assembly, a thorough cleaning is in order after all the machining operations. All plugs should be opened to expose all oil galleys and stiff bristled bottle brushes (or gun cleaning brushes) should be used to thoroughly clean everything. The first scrubbing of the block should be done with solvent, then a second scrubbing with detergent and hot water. Wilson uses a final rinse with steam cleaning equipment. Compressed air is the best method of drying the block, and if it is not available, paper towels should be used. Cloths should never be used as they deposit too much lint. Then, all of the block's machined surfaces should immediately be oiled with WD-40 to prevent rust. If the block is going to be stored for a while before assembly, it should be wrapped tightly in plastic material.

A word about painting the interior of the block: many experts say it helps seal the pores of the block and keep small particles out of the oil. This may be so. But the major problem is that it is difficult to get the block clean enough to insure the paint will adhere properly. When the paint is exposed to very hot oil which is being thrown about inside the block, there is a good possibility that specks, or even strips of paint can peel and become clogged in bearings, the oil pump pickup screen, etc. Wilson's advice: Don't paint it.

Some special notes are in order for modifications on certain blocks:

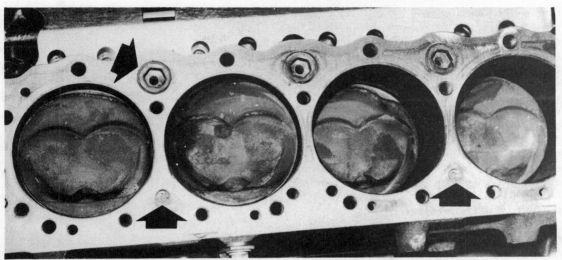

The top three water passages on the Chevy 350 block [see top arrow] are plugged with a 3/4" steel pipe plug, then the plugs are drilled with a 1/4" hole for water flow. The 1/4" passage is all the head gasket allows, so the block holes are brought in line with the gasket to stabilize the block. The bottom arrows point to the holes blocked with the 1/8" steel pipe plugs.

THE CHEVY BLOCK

On the Chevy small block, the water passages on the deck surface between the two intake valves on each side should be tapped and plugged with 1/8" steel pipe plugs. This stops the flow of cold water between the hot parts of the cylinder head. Experience has shown that this is what causes cylinder head cracking in the small block.

Another trick which stabilizes the block on the Chevy 350 is to restrict the diameter of the three large water passage holes at the top of the cylinder bores on each deck. The cylinder head gasket holes which mate to these deck holes are not nearly as large as the block holes, so they may be narrowed. Each hole is tapped and plugged with a 3/4" steel pipe plug. Then 1/4" holes are drilled in the center of the pipe plugs. Be sure to Loctite the pipe plugs when they are installed. This operation makes for much less cylinder wall distortion.

Both the pipe plug operations described here should be done before the deck is cut in the milling machine.

THE MOPAR 340

The Chrysler 340 block comes with only two-bolt main caps. Four-bolt main caps are mandatory in any racing situation. The special four-bolt main caps to fit the 340 are available from Milodon Engineering. They are made of the same material as the block to insure the same expansion rate as the block as it heats. Like any precision machine operation on a high-performance block, their

installation should be done by an experienced machine shop. The outside two bolts on the Milodon main caps are angled outward to be perpendicular with the rod angularity as it receives its major force. When the bolts are installed to the outside two holes of these main caps, silicone rubber adhesive must be liberally squirted into the holes and between the block/cap mating surfaces, as well as around the bolts, because the holes penetrate the water jacket. After the caps are installed, the block must be align-honed.

The 340 block has one oiling shortcoming. That is, the right side main oil galley has too great a pressure running in it, and the passages which feed from it to the main bearings sometimes are starved. This is because the oil flow is so rapid and the oil is forced to make a 90-degree bend. To remedy this problem, Chrysler engineers suggest the following procedure:

Drill or ream the right hand main oil galley to 5/8" diameter. Start from the front of the block and go past four tappet bores. Repeat this operation from the rear of the block and go past four tappet bores (each length is approximately 10 inches). In each of these drilled passages, a tube must be driven in (one from the rear of the block and one from the front). The tube may be copper, aluminum or steel thin wall tubing, 5/8" O.D. and 1/2" I.D. An old tappet, rounded off at the bottom, must be used to peen a dent in the tube through each tappet bore, because the tubes create a small interference with the tappets. Drill all of the oil passages which intersect the galley through the tubes (use a 19/64" drill). Drill the oil passages from the main bearing bulkhead to the oil galleys on the number 1, 2, 3 and 4 mains. Drill the passages from the main bearing bulkhead to the camshaft bearing bores on the number 2 and 4. Drill the passage from the cam bearing bores to the deck of the block on journals 2 and 4 (this is for feeding the rocker shafts). All of these are drilled with the 19/64" drill.

The output oil to the remote oil filter and the return oil from the filter should be separated from each other by a pressed-in plug in the oil passage at the side of the block. This plug is Chrysler part number 3462871. Be sure this plug is pressed into the hole until it bottoms solidly.

Once the restrictor tubes have been placed in the right oil galley, they should be threaded on each end to accept a 1/2" pipe plug.

Because the 340 block is made of a "soft" cast iron material, Chrysler engineers highly recommend that the block be stress relieved. The stress relieving process consists of heating the block and main caps to 1050°F and holding at this temperature for two hours. It should then be furnace cooled to 500°F at a rate not to exceed 200°F per hour. After it has reached 500°F, it can be air cooled. After stress relieving, the cam bearings must be removed and thrown away. The main cap bolts will also have to be replaced. This process should be done before any align honing or any

Notice how the oil galley which feeds the main bearings has been counter-bored ¼" where it makes a sharp turn back up to the cam bearings. This shouldn't be done. It relieves a restriction at the main bearing feed hole, giving the oil an easier path to follow than to the mains.

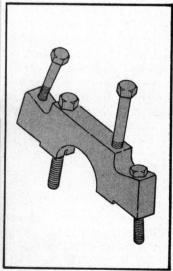

The center three main bearing webs on the Chrysler 340 require four-bolt main caps. Notice how the holes have been drilled at an angle for the outboard bolts on each replacement cap.

The Milodon four-bolt main cap for the Chrysler 340.

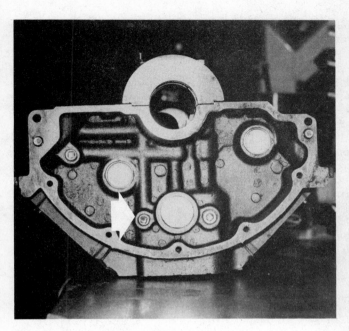

The oil galley [as seen from the rear of the block] which must be drilled oversize and have a restrictor tube placed in it [see arrow].

In addition to the tube insert into the right oil galley of the MoPar 340, the front of the left side main galley should be blocked as the Chrysler drawings show for better oil pressure.

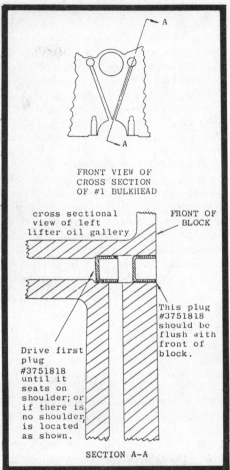

FRONT VIEW OF
CROSS SECTION
OF #1 BULKHEAD

cross sectional view of left lifter oil gallery

FRONT OF BLOCK

This plug #3751818 should be flush with front of block.

Drive first plug #3751818 until it seats on shoulder; or if there is no shoulder is located as shown.

SECTION A-A

From the front of the block the oil galley to be modified can be seen [see arrow].

machine work is carried out.

Chrysler is selling blocks which have already been stress relieved under part number P3690961.

Chrysler also highly recommends that the block you use for any serious racing should be tested for cylinder wall thickness because they have had a problem with core shift. The cylinder wall thickness should be a minimum of .090" in the area between cylinders, and .160" thick (minimum) on the thrust side of the cylinder.

The top two threads of all cylinder head bolts on the 340 should be ground away during the deburring operation to eliminate deck distortion problems which the 340 has encountered. It also helps the rings seal better. Also to aid block to head sealing, Chrysler recommends that head studs replace the stock head bolts.

MAXIMUM OVERBORES

Engine	Maximum Overbore
Chevrolet 350	.030"
Chrysler 340	.010"
Ford 351-C	.030"

THE HEAD GASKET

When installing a head gasket, be sure the head and deck mating surfaces are absolutely clean. Wipe both surfaces down with lacquer thinner to remove any film, grease or small dirt particles which could possibly be detrimental to good sealing.

When installing the head gaskets, be sure to follow the head torquing sequence (shown in drawings in the engine assembly chapter elsewhere in this book). Torque the heads in several increments, gradually working up to the maximum torque. This will keep the gasket smooth—just like ironing pants.

For the Chevrolet 350, the gasket to use is the stainless steel gasket, GM part number 3916336. Use two gaskets per side, in a sandwich. Apply a thin coat of aluminum paint as a sealant.

For the Ford 351-C, the gasket to use is Ford part number D3ZZ-6051-A. This is a high performance gasket developed during Ford's Trans Am racing program. To improve the durability of this gasket from coolant pressure, drill a 5/32" hole in the front of it (refer to drawing for exact location). Do not use any gasket sealant.

Chrysler Corporation has done a lot of work trying to find the answer for head gasket sealing on the 340. This has been one of the biggest problem areas for the 340. Chrysler's latest suggestion is their head gasket number 3698659. There is, however, another gasket under this same part number. Use **only** the one with the source identification number of 61080. This number appears right on the gasket under the part number. Again with this head gasket, do not use any gasket sealant.

If you have serious head gasket problems with the MoPar 340, the only answer is to use O-rings around the cylinder bores. Use stainless steel wire for the O-rings.

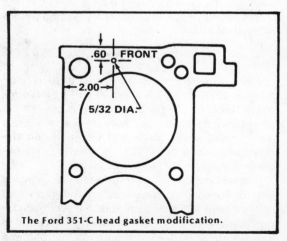

The Ford 351-C head gasket modification.

Ford has a new head gasket (part number M-6051-A341) for use with their new 351 SVO aluminum cylinder heads.

The Lubrication System

The information we present here pertaining to oil pressures and pump modifications will work correctly only if the critical clearance recommendations we present are followed meticuloulsy. Incorrect clearances, such as too much rod and main bearing clearance, will have a drastic effect on proper oil flow and pressure by building in an internal oil leakage.

THE CHEVY 350 OIL PUMP

The pump to use in the Chevy 350 is part number 3969870, which is actually designated for use in the 427. The big block pump is used in the small block because it has more teeth on the gears which reduces the loads and vibrations on the distributor and its driveshaft. A vibrating distributor driveshaft causes spark scatter.

Grooves should be milled into the gear housing interior to equalize pressures on the gears and prevent high RPM oil cavitation (see photos for explanations of areas to be milled). The milled grooves are .050″ deep, cut with a 5/16″ ball end mill in a Bridgeport mill. These grooves can also be cut with a high speed grinder, but it is more time consuming and less accurate. The pump housing is located on the mill table with a fixture keying on the gear shaft hole.

The oil pump body is modified for pressure relief grooves in the Bridgeport mill.

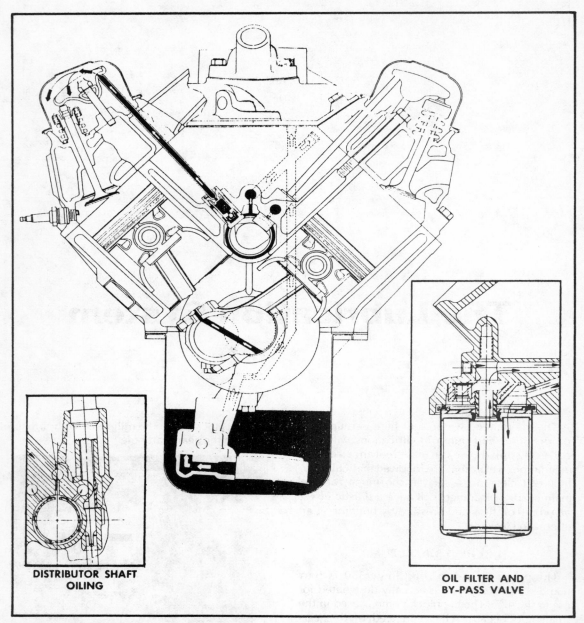

DISTRIBUTOR SHAFT OILING

OIL FILTER AND BY-PASS VALVE

The Chevrolet oiling system.

All interior sharp edges have to be deburred, and sharp edges on the gears are cleaned up with a fine grit cloth. Then the entire pump assembly should be washed and scrubbed thoroughly.

The pressure relief valve spring should be shimmed with two .031" washers for increased pressure. The shims should be placed inside the pressure bypass valve. This is assuming, of course, that an oil cooler is being used with the engine. The hot running oil pressure for a Chevy small block should be 55 PSI, with 60 pounds being an absolute maximum.

The oil pump pickup tube, in stock form, is pressed into the pump body and tack welded. It should be brazed securely with a generous application of brazing material all around the joint.

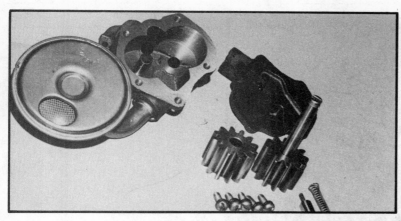

Stock Chevy 427 oil pump [being installed on the 350] before modification for pressure relief.

The heavier duty 427 Chevy oil pump is used in the Chevy small block. The pump cover, left, and body, right, have been grooved with the Bridgeport mill as arrows indicate to balance pressures on gears and pump driveshaft. This is important to assure pump durability.

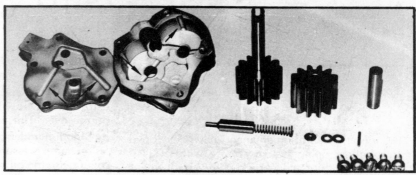

Notice support plate which has been brazed to oil pump pick-up...good insurance to protect the oil source!

THE FORD 351-C OIL PUMP

The stock Ford 351-C oil pump, part number M-6600-C3, should be used. With it use oil pump pickup screen number M-6622-A302. A heavier duty oil pump driveshaft is required, and is found under Ford part number M-6605-A351.

No modification to the Ford 351-C oiling system or pump is required, regardless of what many magazine stories have said. Wilson has built many Ford 351-C engines with the lubrication system as outlined here, and they have survived thousands of NASCAR superspeedway racing miles without failure.

Use the stock oil pressure relief spring, and shim it with two 3/8 SAE flat washers. This should bring the hot oil operating pressure to 80 PSI. The Ford 351-C needs to operate with no less than 75 to 85 pounds of oil pressure. Or use kit #M-6670-351.

The pickup tube in the Ford engine threads into the pump housing and has a tendency to break off at the threads because of vibration. The pickup tube should be strengthened in this area by generously brazing the tube to the housing. If a longer than stock pickup tube is required for a deep sump oil pan, get one from a Ford truck engine

The Ford 351-C lubrication system.

(Ford trucks use deep sump pans).

THE MOPAR 340 OIL PUMP

Chrysler Corporation engineers have developed an excellent oiling system for use with the 340 engine. It features a dual pickup line arrangement which significantly improves the gallons per minute capacity of the pump above 5500 RPM. The pump to use is part number 2806270. Inside, the 426 Hemi gear and rotor should be installed for extra oil volume. This also necessitates a larger pump cover. The gears and cover are sold as a set by Milodon under part number 19050. Use Chrysler oil pump pressure relief spring number 3690716 to increase the oil pressure. The 340's hot running oil pressure should be 65 to 70 PSI. The oil pickup is Chrysler part number 3690784, and is connected by two lengths of steel braided hose, part number

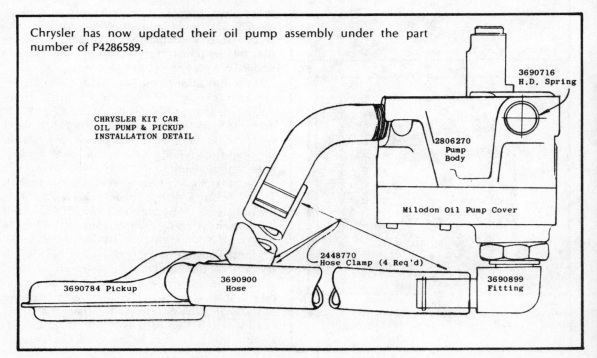

Chrysler has now updated their oil pump assembly under the part number of P4286589.

CHRYSLER KIT CAR
OIL PUMP & PICKUP
INSTALLATION DETAIL

3690716
H.D. Spring

2806270
Pump
Body

Milodon Oil Pump Cover

2448770
Hose Clamp (4 Req'd)

3690784 Pickup

3690900
Hose

3690899
Fitting

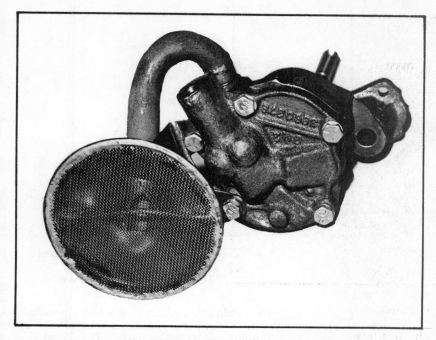

The oil pump pick-up has been modified with a full screen to aid flow into pump. Notice how a bracing rod has been brazed in place to prevent screen from collapsing inward onto pump intake tube. All bolts in pump have been Loctited before assembly.

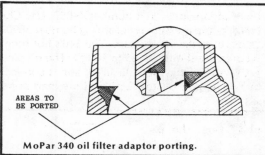

MoPar 340 oil filter adaptor porting.

3690900. See the Chrysler drawings for clarification on everything.

The stock 340 oil pump dirveshaft is not strong enough, so they have introduced a new shaft, part number P3690715. It also includes the drive gear.

The 340's stock oil filter base forces the oil to make a 90° bend, causing a pressure restriction. These offset holes should be ported with a hand grinder as the accompanying illustrations show.

WINDAGE TRAYS

The windage tray is a sheet metal baffle which is bolted to the main caps and separates the crankshaft from the oil sump in the bottom of the engine. The tray prevents frictional horsepower loss from the crankshaft operating in oil. It also skims the oil off the crank and prevents oil from splashing onto the crank during acceleration. Without the use of a windage tray, it is entirely possible for several quarts of oil to be picked up out of the sump and whipped into a fog by the crank. This creates an extreme frictional drag on the crank, and in addition introduces air into the oiling system.

The stock Chrysler 340 gear and rotor is shown at left and the Hemi 426 part is at right.

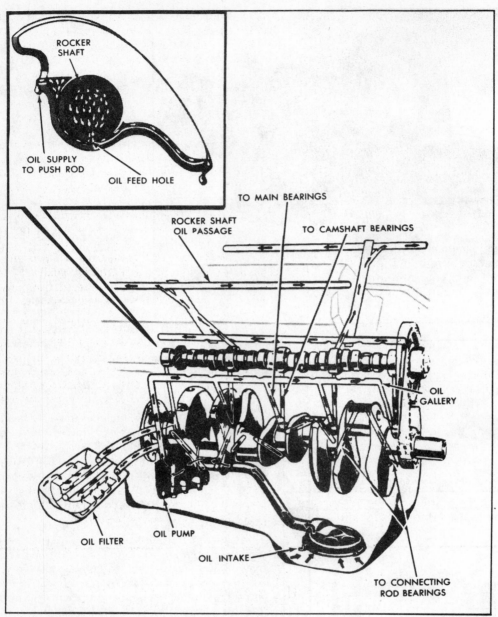

ROCKER
SHAFT

OIL SUPPLY
TO PUSH ROD

OIL FEED HOLE

TO MAIN BEARINGS

ROCKER SHAFT
OIL PASSAGE

TO CAMSHAFT BEARINGS

OIL
GALLERY

OIL FILTER

OIL PUMP

OIL INTAKE

TO CONNECTING
ROD BEARINGS

The Chrysler 340 lubrication system.

PUMP PICKUP LOCATION

The oil pump pickup should be located in the position where it has the best chance of being immersed in oil at all times. On oval track cars turning left, this would be on the right rear side of the oil pan. Additional baffling in the oil pan should position the oil so it cannot escape from around the pickup tube as the car accelerates and brakes. The pickup opening should be positioned from 1/4" to 3/8" above the oil pan floor.

WHICH OIL TO USE

There is only one type of oil to use in a competition engine: a non-foaming, ashless high performance oil. The weight should be 20W-50. There are many companies making an oil of this type--Union, Valvoline, Quaker State, Pennzoil and Kendall, to name a few.

Typical of the windage trays is this one made by Chevrolet. The front two windage tray attachment bolts on the Chevy 350 must be ground off shorter so they do not contact oil pan.

The oil should be run at around 200 degrees. If your oil temperature consistantly gets higher than this, a larger capacity cooler is in order.

The minimum capacity for any high performance engine is 8 quarts of oil. Any less than this will allow the oil to heat up too much.

GAUGES

Two gauges relating to the oiling system are mandatory for the protection of the engine: an oil temperature gauge and an oil pressure gauge.

The oil temperature which you want to check is the oil which is going to the bearings after filtering and cooling. The temperature gauge, then, should be placed anywhere in the oil line after the cooler. Many coolers have a provision for a temperature sending unit in the oil output line from the cooler.

The oil pressure which you want to check is that which is feeding the bearings, so the oil pressure line should be tapped into the block in an oil galley which is feeding the main bearings. The oil pressure gauge line should be a minimum of 1/8" ID to get a good gauge response and help detect any oil pressure losses quickly.

The majority of engine bearing failures are a direct result of oil pressure loss due to the oil pump picking up air while the car is negotiating turns at speed. This occurs at a time when the driver is busiest and may go unreported, or be reported as a slight drop in oil pressure in the turns. Good gauge response is necessary to trouble shoot this problem and the gauge should be mounted as close to the driver's line of vision as is practical.

Oil pressure loss in turns is aggravated by three things: 1) Insufficient oil level or capacity, 2) High engine oil flow rates due to excessive bearing clearances, or higher than necessary oil pressure, and 3) Improper oil pan baffling, usually over-baffling which prevents the engine oil from properly draining back into the oil pan while the car is in a turn.

Another frequent cause of lost oil pressure in an oiling system is the excessive use of 90° fittings in the lines. They are a difinite pressure restriction. Try to use all 45° fittings. Another pressure loss problem is caused by the use of two coolers and/or two filters. These units, in pairs, are not necessary.

OIL ROUTING

The proper routing of oil lines for a wet sump engine is from the engine to the filter to the cooler and back to the engine. It is preferable for the oil to be filtered before cooling so as much debris as possible can be kept out of the cooler.

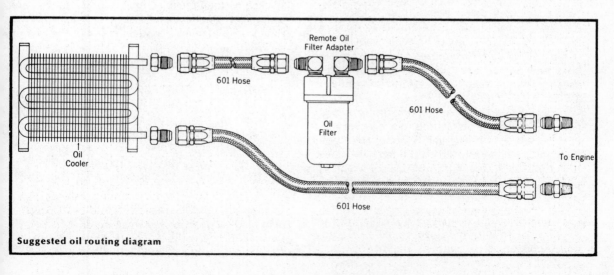

Remote Oil Filter Adapter

601 Hose

Oil Filter

601 Hose

To Engine

Oil Cooler

601 Hose

Suggested oil routing diagram

A great example of how not to do it! Don't ever put an oil radiator in front of a water radiator. It kills the cooling efficiency of both radiators.

In case your engine blows, this entire oil routing system must be thoroughly cleaned before running a new engine again. We know of one driver who blew seven engines in a row because he did not think to clean his cooler out after he lost the first engine.

The cooler must be emptied, thoroughly drained with solvent, then 3 to 4 clean quarts of oil should be poured through it. The same goes for the oil lines. They should be thoroughly cleaned with solvent or steam, then new oil should be run through them before installing.

THE OIL COOLER

With the type of performance being expected out of a competition engine today, an oil cooler is mandatory. There are many brands on the market, and many large aircraft type coolers are also available from aircraft surplus stores.

One of the most widely used coolers is the Harrison part number 3157804. It is a little more expensive than some which are available from oil cooler specialty companies, but it is known for getting the job done. The Harrison cooler is available from Chevrolet parts departments.

At least ½" ID oil lines, preferably steel braided lines such as the Aeroquip 601 hose, should be used for routing the oil to and from the engine and cooler.

When you get a new cooler, do not just install it right out of the box, but rather clean it out as we outlined above. Once this is done, the cooler, filter and all oil lines should be filled with new oil before they are attached to the engine. This can eliminate early bearing failure problems.

THE DRY SUMP SYSTEM

So far in this lubrication chapter, we have concerned ourselves with stock-type oil pumps and the wet sump system. A wet sump, basically, is the type of lubrication system which is supplied on virtually all passenger automobiles, where the oil storage is in a sump under the engine, and a two-stage pump is driven off the camshaft. This pump draws oil from the reservoir sump (or oil pan) and then pushes, or pumps, it under pressure throughout the various oil galleys to lubricate the bearings and other essential parts. Oil return to the sump is by downward gravity flow.

The dry sump system eliminates some of the inherent problems of the wet sump. First of all, the stock oil pump and its drive from the cam are eliminated. The pump is externally mounted and drives off the crankshaft. The pressure pump pulls the oil out of an externally mounted oil reservoir tank and pushes it under pressure into the engine oil galleys.

The dry sump pump is a multi-stage pump, one for the pressure feed to the engine and three stages for scavenging, or sucking, the oil out of the engine. The best current arrangement for the scavenge pump pickups, for oval track racing, are one each at the front and rear of the oil pan on the right side, and one stage sucking out of the rear of the right side cylinder head. These scavenging stages pull the oil out of the engine and return it to the reservoir tank.

There are five major reasons for using a dry sump system: (1) More effective and thorough lubrication, (2) A more constant supply of oil regardless of vehicle attitude, (3) Better oil cooling, (4) Eliminating torsional stress loads which the oil pump places on the camshaft and distributor, (5) Elimination of the large oil sump under engine so the engine and chassis can be lowered.

The most effective dry sump system, as we said, is the four stage unit. There are also three stage units on the market, which have two scavenging stages and one pressure stage. There is one

A Chrysler 340 engine with a Weaver Brothers four-stage dry sump pump visible at lower left. Scavenging hoses extend under pan. Notice how distributor cap is numbered for quick reference.

more dry sump system available, but it has several inherent disadvantages. This is the one-stage system. It employs the stock oil pump for pressure feed to the engine, with the one-stage scavenge pump keeping the pan dry.

The major problem with the one-stage dry sump is that the stock oil pump is still used, and the torsional loads on the cam and distributor are still present. The other problem is that the scavenge pump does not operate at sufficient volume to keep the pan dry and the crank from operating in a film of oil.

With the advent of many NASCAR racers using dry sump systems with the small block engines, Chevrolet engineers issued a several-point checklist of their ideas which will help promote the system's successful operation:

1) The scavenge pumps, in order to keep the engine from filling up with a backlog of oil, should have three times the capacity of the pressure pump.

2) Two of the scavenging stages should draw oil from the pan, and a third stage should be connected to the rear outside corner of the rocker cover on the predominant outboard side of the car (for oval tracks, this means the right rear corner of the

engine). Wilson has improved this suggestion one better by connecting the third stage pickup to the rear of the right side cylinder head in the oil drainback area.

3) Use a minimum of 3/4'' ID lines from the pump to the reservoir tank, and from the tank to the pressure pump. The high pressure oil routing

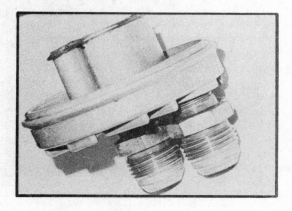

This engine oil adapter, machined from aluminum, is sold by Junior Johnson Associates in Ronda, North Carolina. It threads into oil filter adapter and provides access for exterior oil lines to and from cooler and filter.

Pipe fitting at upper right of head attaches to a scavenging stage of the dry sump system. It evacuates oil waiting to drain back to the sump which accumulates at the outboard corner.

lines should be at least ½" ID.

4) The oil should be routed from the pan to the scavenge pump to the reservoir tank to the filter to the cooler to the engine oil galleys.

5) Do not run the oil pressure too high. If it is, it will aggravate good scavenging and oil aeration.

6) The reservoir tank should be as tall as possible and as small in diameter as possible. The tank should hold a minimum of two gallons of oil with air space above the oil for proper pressure venting. The line returning oil to the tank should have a course screen type of filter. The bottom of the tank should be at least as high or higher from the ground than the pressure pump intake to assure gravity priming of the pump.

7) Vent the engine from breather holes in the valve covers at their front uppermost point. Use a ¾" ID line on the upper left rear side of the valve cover to the top of the reservoir tank.

There are on the market many different types of dry sump oil pans with special pickups and a shallow depth. They are, to be sure, useful, but they are also costly. Many NASCAR Grand National racers have found that the stock engine pan works just great, with the pickups brazed into the center of the sump and securely attached. Of the special aftermarket variety of pans, the most successful is the type which is shallowest at the center and drains downhill to the front and to the rear of the engine, with a scavenge pump pickup attached at the deepest point in the front and the rear.

The oil filter adapter on this MoPar 340 has been plugged and holes for a remote oil filter connection have been drilled and tapped.

Note: Proper oil filtering for a high performance engine is critical. Use a Fram HP1 filter, and change it religiously.

An increasing number of engine builders are placing stainless steel screen over the oil drainback holes in the block to prevent debris from going back to the pan and the pump. Screen kits are available from Phil Henny.

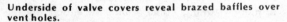

Underside of valve covers reveal brazed baffles over vent holes.

If rags are required around the breather caps, something is wrong. There is either a blow-by or drain-back problem. The best solution is to fix it not block it. Notice how clean engine compartment appears with steel braided hoses. They cost more initially, but give better service.

The Induction System

You've heard it said many times that an engine is basically an air pump. The more air and fuel which is pumped into it, the more power the engine will put out. That is why engine performance tuning concentrates so much on the breathing ability of the engine. The cam timing, valve size and shape and combustion chamber intake runner shape all affect the breathing. But before any of these elements can have a chance at improving performance, the air and fuel have to be inducted through the carburetor and intake manifold.

CARBURETOR BASICS

The carburetor, as complex as it appears, is little more than a small barrel through which a stream of air passes and picks up miniscule drops of fuel. The air stream is caused by atmospheric pressure which pushes air in to take the place of the vacuum created by the intake stroke of the pistons.

When an engine can consume all of the oxygen in the air/fuel mixture which it draws in, maximum power output is achieved. The ideal air/fuel mixture for this burning is 14.8 parts of air to one part of fuel. But in the environment of the engine, this mixture ratio has to be between 12:1 and 13:1.

These are the ratios which are changed when metering jet sizes are being changed.

Air flow capacity (measured in cubic feet per minute or CFM) can aid the performance of an engine, but remember these important facts: Several small barrels, or venturis, will yield a better torque curve than a few large venturis. This is because air velocity is faster through a smaller diameter opening. This is why the right carburetor is important for the specific application. Each venturi size has a purpose. Having large venturis open while accelerating at a low RPM range momentarily decreases the air flow speed, causing what is called a "flat spot." Smaller venturis eliminate this problem.

An example of this would be two identical Chevelle sportsman cars powered by a 350 engine. One has a 650 CFM carburetor, the other a 1050 CFM. They both accelerate off a tight turn on a quarter-mile track. All other factors being equal, the car with the 650 CFM carb will beat the other one every time because of the smaller venturis creating a greater air flow velocity. The car with the 1050 CFM will experience a continuous flat spot until the engine catches up to the carburetor's operating peak, and this will most likely be at the

TYPICAL VIEW HOLLEY CARBURETOR MODELS 3160, 4150 & 4160

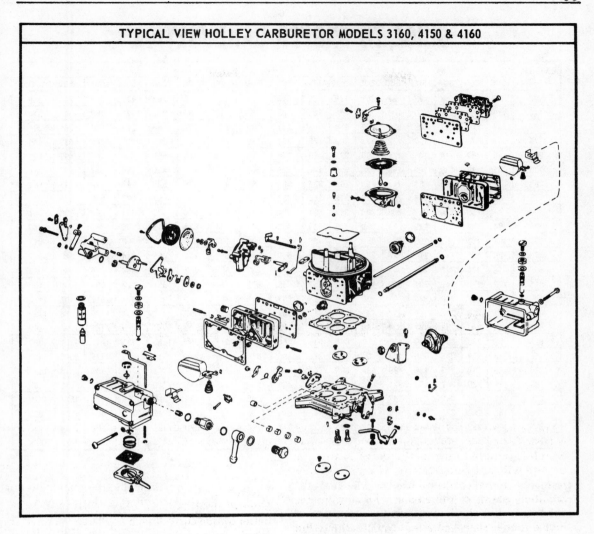

very end of the straightaway.

Over-carburetion (having too much CFM capacity) will hurt the performance of a car much more than having too small a carburetor, especially in the low and mid-RPM ranges. The engine needs the high air velocity to atomize the fuel. Many people think the larger the better, but it just isn't so. Consult the carburetion guide (which is provided courtesy of Offenhauser manifolds). It will give you an idea of the CFM capacity needed for the cubic inch displacement of your engine, at its maximum RPM range. Note that the table is about 10 percent conservative.

THE HOLLEY CARBURETOR

For high performance competition, the Holley carburetor is far and away the winner's choice. It is a well-built, easily tuned carb. For any competi-

tion use, the only model to consider is one of Holley's 4150 double pumpers. These feature center inlet dual feed fuel bowls, double accelerator pumps and mechanical secondaries. The center inlet fuel bowls help to control fuel starvation while the vehicle is experiencing hard cornering These carburetors, with part numbers listed in a table, are the only ones we will be considering here.

The Holley carburetors have four fuel metering systems: 1) the idle system, 2) the accelerator pump system, 3) the main metering system, and 4) the power enrichment system.

At idle, the engine has a very high manifold vacuum but there is very little air velocity being drawn into the carburetor. This means the air flow is not great enough to draw enough fuel out of the main metering system to sustain engine idle. Thus,

GUIDE TO PROPER CARBURETION

ENGINE C.I.D.	ENGINE R.P.M.																
	1000	1500	2000	2500	3000	3500	4000	4500	5000	5500	6000	6500	7000	7500	8000	8500	9000
100	29	44	58	72	87	101	116	130	145	159	174	188	203	217	231	246	260
125	36	54	72	90	109	127	145	163	181	199	217	235	253	271	289	307	326
150	43	65	87	109	130	152	174	195	217	239	260	282	304	326	347	369	391
175	51	76	101	127	152	177	203	228	253	279	304	329	354	379	405	430	456
200	58	87	116	145	174	203	231	260	289	318	347	376	405	434	463	492	521
225	65	98	130	163	195	228	260	293	326	358	391	423	456	488	521	553	586
250	72	109	145	181	217	253	289	326	362	398	434	470	506	543	579	615	651
275	80	119	159	199	239	279	318	358	398	438	477	517	557	597	637	676	716
300	87	130	174	217	260	304	347	391	434	477	521	564	608	651	694	738	781
325	94	141	188	235	282	329	376	423	470	517	564	611	658	705	752	799	846
350	101	152	203	253	304	354	405	456	506	557	608	658	709	760	810	861	911
375	109	163	217	271	326	380	434	488	543	597	651	705	760	814	868	922	977
400	116	174	231	289	347	405	463	521	579	637	694	752	810	868	926	984	1042
425	123	184	246	307	369	430	492	553	615	676	738	799	861	922	984	1045	1107
450	130	195	260	326	391	456	521	586	651	716	781	846	911	977	1042	1107	1172
475	137	206	275	344	412	481	550	618	687	756	825	893	962	1031	1100	1168	1237
500	145	217	289	362	434	506	579	651	723	796	868	940	1013	1085	1157	1230	1302
525	152	228	304	380	456	532	608	684	760	836	911	987	1063	1139	1215	1291	1367
550	159	239	318	398	477	557	637	716	796	875	955	1034	1114	1194	1273	1353	1432
575	166	250	333	416	499	582	666	749	832	915	998	1081	1165	1248	1331	1414	1497
600	174	260	347	434	521	608	694	781	868	955	1042	1128	1215	1302	1389	1476	1563
625	181	271	362	452	543	633	723	814	904	995	1085	1175	1266	1356	1447	1537	1628
650	188	282	376	470	564	658	752	846	940	1034	1128	1223	1317	1411	1505	1599	1693
675	195	293	391	488	586	684	781	879	977	1074	1172	1270	1367	1465	1563	1660	1758
700	203	304	405	506	608	709	810	911	1013	1114	1215	1317	1418	1519	1620	1722	1823

the high manifold vacuum is used to draw fuel out of the idle circuit. It is atomized with air from air bleeds.

When a car is accelerated, especially with wide open throttle, the carburetor butterflies open wide and there is a great rush of air. But air is lighter than gasoline, so it rushes in faster than fuel. This causes a momentarily very lean mixture. To cover this "catch up" period, the accelerator pump system comes into action. It is connected by a mechanical linkage to the throttle linkage, and as the throttle is mashed, the accelerator pumps shoot a measured shot of raw gasoline into the air stream entering the venturis.

The main metering system comes into play when the throttle is open wide enough to allow a fast stream of air through the venturis. It is here the venturis create a vacuum which draws fuel out of the bowl.

The power valve system supplies a richer mixture for full power operation. When the manifold vacuum drops to a certain level, the engine is requiring a richer mixture than the main metering system is providing. Basically, the main metering system is a very lean circuit. The power valves supply the balance of the required fuel. Holley power valves are numbered according to the amount of vacuum required to operate them. For example, if a number 65 power valve is installed then the vacuum has to drop to 6.5 inches of mercury (plus or minus .5") for the power valve to operate.

SETTING UP THE HOLLEY DOUBLE PUMPER

The following tips from Waddell Wilson are the benefit of his more than 20 years of engine building and tuning experience. Many people think there are many "trick" modifications which can be done to the Holley to make it perform better. As Wilson puts it though, "The Holley is a good, sound carburetor just as it comes out of the box. Only a few minor changes are necessary, along with careful inspection to see that the carburetor has been manufactured to specifucations."

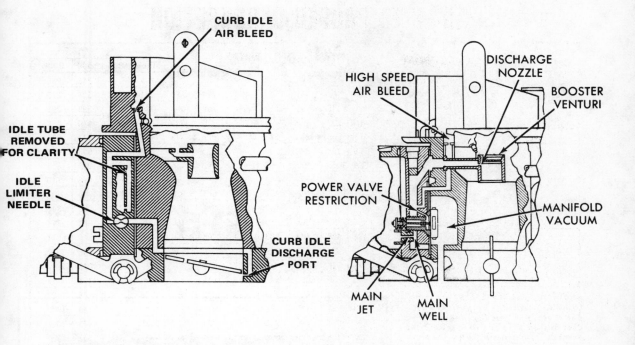

CURB IDLE
AIR BLEED

IDLE TUBE
REMOVED
FOR CLARITY

IDLE
LIMITER
NEEDLE

CURB IDLE
DISCHARGE
PORT

Curb Idle System

HIGH SPEED
AIR BLEED

DISCHARGE
NOZZLE

BOOSTER
VENTURI

POWER VALVE
RESTRICTION

MANIFOLD
VACUUM

MAIN
JET

MAIN
WELL

Power Enrichment System

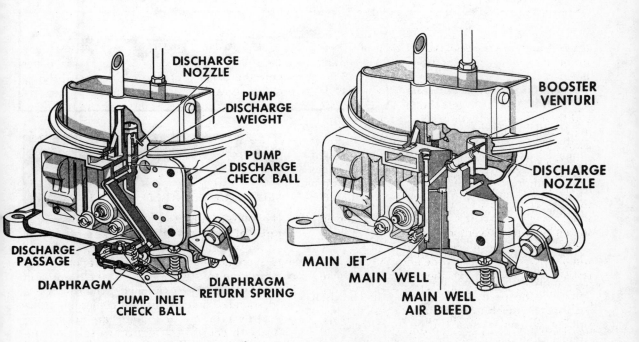

DISCHARGE
NOZZLE

PUMP
DISCHARGE
WEIGHT

PUMP
DISCHARGE
CHECK BALL

DISCHARGE
PASSAGE

DIAPHRAGM

PUMP INLET
CHECK BALL

DIAPHRAGM
RETURN SPRING

Accelerator Pump System

BOOSTER
VENTURI

DISCHARGE
NOZZLE

MAIN JET

MAIN WELL

MAIN WELL
AIR BLEED

Main Metering System

Above, the Holley 830 CFM, ready to be assembled. Be sure that all parts are periodically soaked and cleaned to prevent dirt, gum and varnish formations. These accumulations can block the small air bleed passages.

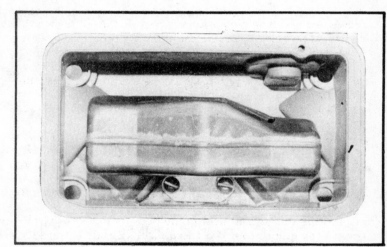

At right, The proper float setting for the front fuel bowl.

The first step is to cut the choke tower off flush with the top of the carburetor air horn. This tower impedes air flow into the carburetor, especially if there is a clearance problem. Grind all sharp edges down smooth. This process can be done on a Bridgeport mill, or with a hacksaw and file. For competition engines, the entire choke assembly which comes with the carburetor should also be discarded. Use silicone rubber to block off the choke lever opening in the carburetor body.

Another part which can be discarded before assembly is the sintered bronze fuel filters which fit inside the fuel inlet on each of the fuel bowls. It won't take much to stop one of these up. In its place, you must use an inline fuel filter with a replaceable paper cartridge element. Don't ever run without a clean fuel filter.

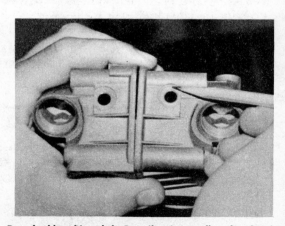

Rear fuel bowl is at left. Pencil points to float level sight plug hole.

Wilson demonstrates use of his booster tightening vise.

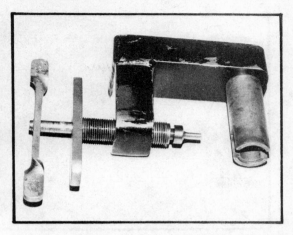

This is the vise used to straighten and tighten venturi boosters.

The first assembly is the fuel bowls. After inserting the float into the bowl, be sure the float moves freely with no bind. Also, use a small, fine-calibrated measure to be sure the float is setting level in the bowl.

Next, install the needle and seat. The only needle and seat to use is the .110 size seat with a viton needle, Holley part number 18BP-135AS. Put a small amount of oil on the o-ring on the needle and seat before installing it.

With the bowls inverted, line up the front fuel bowl float bottom even with the height of the top of the screws at the rear of the bowl. In the rear bowl, the bottom of the float should be 3/32" above the top of the screws.

In the main carburetor body, the venturi boost-ers must be straight and tight in the body. Many times they come from the factory loose and cocked. Loose, or cocked, boosters can cause the carburetor to run lean. Wilson uses a special vise tool he constructed to properly locate and tighten the boosters.

The fuel bowl atmospheric vent tubes must be altered in length, according to the air cleaner housing to be used. The top of the tubes should be

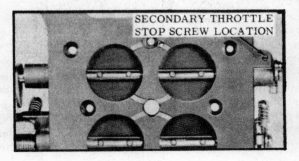

SECONDARY THROTTLE STOP SCREW LOCATION

cut to fall 3/4" below the cleaner housing. If they are any closer, the fuel level in the bowls could be affected, thus causing the engine miss or run rich.

The only power valve to use in competition carburetors is the 6-hole outlet number 65. The Holley part number is 25BP-400A-65. Do not run the carburetor without the power valve.

Once the base is installed on the main body and the linkage is hooked up, be sure that both the primary and secondary butterflies are open the same amount, and all the way, at full throttle. It is common to sometimes see the secondaries slight-ly angled when the primaries are wide open. If this is the case on your carburetor, bend the linkage rod gently to compensate.

Always check the adjustment on the secondary butterfly opening. To adjust, back off on the adjusting screw until the butterflies close, then run the adjusting screw in ½ turn.

There are two sizes of accelerator pumps which can be installed, 25 cc and 50 cc. The carburetor comes with the 25 cc model on the primary side. On the 700, 800 and 850 CFM models, 50 cc pumps are equipped on the secondary side. If you want to install the 50 cc shot, order Holley part number 85BP-3354. The larger accelerator pump should be used with box-type manifolds on both primary and secondary sides. If you use the 50 cc pump, a ¼" thick spacer must be used under the carburetor base for clearance in some cases.

Get the Holley accelerator pump cam kit num-ber 85BP-3186. From this kit, use the white cam. The plate on the accelerator pump linkage has two holes marked "1" and "2". Install the cams in the number "2" holes. These cams control the metering rate at which the accelerator pump slug

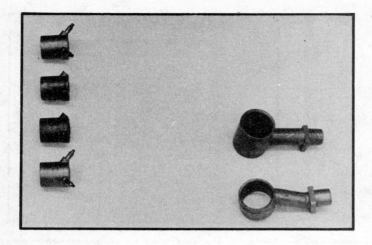

Four different Holley accelerator pump shooter sizes are illustrated at the left, and two different size boosters are shown at right.

of fuel is fed into the carburetor. Use this cam set-up on both primary and secondary sides of all Holley double pumpers.

There are six sizes of accelerator pump discharge nozzles available: .021″, .025″, .026″, .028″, .031″, and .035″. They can be used to tailor the metering of the accelerator pump shot to cover a flat spot in the carburetion. If your car has a slight hesitation, for instance, when you accelerate, and the carburetor has #25 nozzles, switch to #28s or #31s. If the nozzles in your carb are too big, then the response will not be snappy when you accelerate and you will probably notice a puff of black smoke from the exhaust.

A stumble or bog can be caused by a lean or a rich pump shot. The engine will sometimes backfire if extremely lean, but trial and error is usually the best cure with different shooter sizes. Tailoring the idle system will also cure an off-idle bog.

Be sure the accelerator pump lever has some play in it when the throttle blades are wide open. Hold the throttle wide open and the pump operating lever in a fully compressed position. The clearance between the adjusting nut and the pump lever should be .015″. The clearance is vital.

To bench-adjust the idle, seat the idle adjusting needle lightly and back off 2 turns. Readjust to proper idle speed and mixture when the engine has been brought up to operating temperature. Keep both the primary and secondary sides equal. You should try to keep the idle mixture lean to prevent plug fouling.

After the carburetor has been installed and the engine is operating, the float adjustment can be double checked. With the car on a level surface and the engine running, take the screw out of the fuel bowl sight plug. The fuel level should be right at the threads at the bottom of the sight plug port.

If the level needs to be adjusted, the adjusting nut turned clockwise lowers the level, and the nut turned counter-clockwise raises it. Be sure the adjusting nut is held firmly in place with a wrench while the lockscrew is being retightened.

1 TO1 LINKAGE

There are two types of linkages which connect the primary butterflies to the secondary butterflies: progressive and one-to-one. All Holley performance models come equipped with the progressive linkage. This linkage allows the primaries to open one third of the way before the secondaries begin to crack open. This is a method which allows good air flow velocity at low RPMs. With one-to-one linkage, both the primaries and secondaries open simultaneously.

One-to-one linkage is used widely in superspeedway applications where the RPM range is high already when the throttle is mashed to the floor. With one-to-one linkage on a carburetor for short track racing, most drivers find the response hard to control. Progressive linkage is best for short track racing.

To convert any carburetor to one-to-one linkage, use Holley kit number 85R-4704.

If one-to-one linkage is used, larger accelerator pump discharge nozzles should also be used.

JETTING

In the accompanying table of Holley performance carburetor specifications, you can note which jets the various models are equipped with as they come from the factory.

If you do not have a close idea of which jetting to use, it is best to start conservatively with the jets which come in the carburetor. Judge the

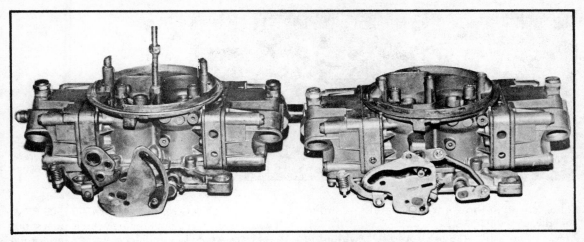

Carburetor at left has one-to-one linkage, while at right is a carb with progressive linkage.

appearance of the spark plugs to determine whether leaner or richer jets are in order. (How to read the spark plug coloring is explained in full in the ignition chapter of this book.)

Sometimes you will find it necessary to use "stagger jetting." That is, using different size jets in different positions in the carburetor. Again, the spark plug coloring will be the final determinant in the fine tuning. It has been determined in dyno testing that because of air flow velocity through different manifolds and different types of intake port shapes, some cylinders on some engines will have to be fed with richer mixtures than others.

When starting to run with an unknown engine set-up, be sure to watch the water temperature gauge. When an engine is running too lean, a gain in water temperature will be noticed.

A tip for you if you are running aluminum cylinder heads: they tend to lean out the air/fuel mixture. To be safe with aluminum heads, start with one jet richer all around.

Holley carburetors are jetted with conditions assumed to be at sea level and 70 degrees outside temperature. As a rule of thumb, for each 2000 feet increase in altitude, the jets should be one jet size leaner. For every 40-degree change above 70 degrees F, the jets should also be one jet size leaner.

PUMPS, GAUGES AND LINES

Wilson has found that the Carter brand of fuel pumps are best when a mechanical, on-the-engine fuel pump must be used. They have proven them-

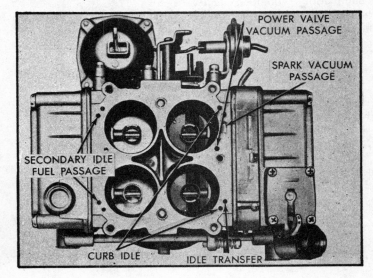

POWER VALVE
VACUUM PASSAGE

SPARK VACUUM
PASSAGE

SECONDARY IDLE
FUEL PASSAGE

CURB IDLE   IDLE TRANSFER

The Holly 830 CFM with LeMans-type fuel bowls is shown here atop Richard Petty's 355 cu. in. small block MoPar.

selves through thousands of high RPM super-speedway racing miles.

A fuel pressure gauge should be a valuable instrument on your instrument panel. The fuel pressure, as delivered to the carburetor, should be seven PSI. If it is too low, problems will result. The fuel pressure gauge should be installed in the fuel line **after** the fuel filter so there is an immediate indication if the fuel line or filter becomes clogged or restricted. Fuel volume is also very important. 50 gallons per hour is the required rate for a small block engine.

Fuel lines should be at least 3/8-inch inside diameter. The best flexible type of fuel line to use is a steel braided line such as Aeroquip 601. This line has a tough double braided exterior and the interior is a synthetic rubber compound which resists contact with any type of fuel. To keep the fuel flowing gracefully, be sure that no 90-degree fittings are used. To keep the fuel cool, route the fuel line away from exhaust pipes, water hoses, oil lines, etc. If the fuel line must pass near any of these hot spots, wrap it in asbestos. Aeroquip also has a special asbestos-type wrapping which they sell called Firesleeve 624. It reduces the penetration of heat to the fuel. In case of a fire, it retards burning.

THE INTAKE MANIFOLD

Choosing the right intake manifold for the right engine and application is as important as any combined operations performed to a competition engine.

Through dyno testing and on-the-track performance, Wilson has found that the following intake manifolds are the best: 1) For the Chevrolet small block, the Edelbrock Victor, 2) For the Ford 351-C, the Edelbrock Scorpion, and 3) For the Chrysler 340, the Edelbrock LD-340.

These manifold recommendations are for engines which generally run from 4500-7500 RPM. If you are operating your racing vehicle on a short, tight track where low-end acceleration and torque are most important, then try these: 1) For the Chevy 350, the Edelbrock Victor Jr., 2) For the Ford 351-C, the Edelbrock Torker, 3) No change for the MoPar 340.

The difference between the Edelbrock Scorpion and Torker manifolds is in their runner configuration and plenum area. Intake manifold runners work, in principle of length/diameter relationship, just like headers. Longer, narrower intake runners help to provide greater torque at lower RPM ranges.

There are few modifications to be performed on an intake manifold of the X-type. The rough casting surfaces of the floor and runners should be ground smooth, but not polished. Do not remove the distribution dams or change the port configurations. Some roughness in the walls of the casting is desired for turbulence. The only time you want the runners polished is with a blower-equipped engine.

For the LD-340 manifold, Chrysler engineers have worked out some modifications which improve fuel/air flow. These modifications must be complemented by using the part number PE71315 air inlet housing. The divider wall of the manifold which divides the left and right sides should be machined away, down to ½-inch from the bottom of the upper manifold floor (see diagram).

To go with these changes, a simple modification must be made in the Holley carburetor main metering bodies. The channel which flows from the power valve to the primary metering jet must be increased to .093-inch in diameter. Use jets #76 in the primaries, and #85 in the secondaries.

A note about box manifolds, such as the Edelbrock Smoky Ram or the Bud Moore Ford manifold. In general, they have some distribution problems. When the throttle is mashed down to

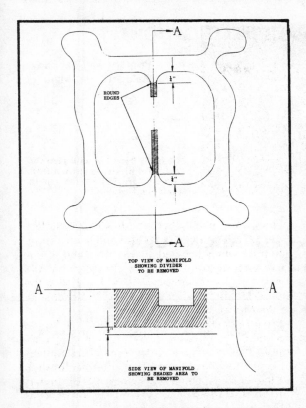

ROUND EDGES

TOP VIEW OF MANIFOLD
SHOWING DIVIDER
TO BE REMOVED

SIDE VIEW OF MANIFOLD
SHOWING SHADED AREA TO
BE REMOVED

accelerate, the response will feel dead. To eliminate this, 50 cc accelerator pumps can be fitted to the carburetor. Also use #35 accelerator pump discharge nozzles with the box manifolds.

An Edelbrock manifold which has been cleaned and deburred in the ports. Ports have also been matched to the head port openings.

With 2″ spacer: 4 individual holes helps the bottom end torque. If the spacer has just an open center, the top end is helped more. A one-inch tall spacer should be run with an open inside. It doesn't hurt bottom end and it helps the top end. Any spacer changes velocity of mixture.

HOLLEY DOUBLE PUMPER SPECIFICATIONS

Holley Part #	CFM	Repair Kit #	Needle & Seat Size	Power Valve	Primary Main Jet	Secondary Main Jet
R4776 AAA	600	37-488	.110	65	69	71
R4777 AAA	650	"	.110	65	71	76
R4778 AAA	700	37-489	.110	85	66	71
R4779 AAA	750	"	.110	85	75	76
R4780 AAA	800	"	.110	65, 85	72	72
R4781 AAA	850	37-485	.110	65	80	80
R4788 AAA	830	37-485	.110	65	80	80

INTAKE MANIFOLD APPLICATION GUIDE

RPM OPERATIONAL RANGE

Engine	4500-6500	5500-6500	5000-7000
Chevy 350	Torker	Victor Jr.	Victor 4+4
Chrysler 340	Victor 340	Victor 340*	Victor 340*
Ford 351-C	Torker 351	Torker 351	Torker 351

Note 1: All of these part numbers are Edelbrock manifolds.
Note 2: For ¼-mile track application with these manifolds, use a Holley 800 CFM carburetor. For greater length tracks, use Holley 830 or 850 CFM carburetors.

*If Chrysler 340 W-2 heads are used, use the Victor W-2 intake manifold.

An Edelbrock Scorpion manifold with walls and plenum floor ground smooth.

The Camshaft

Undoubtedly the most discussed and the most theoretical component in the modern high performance engine is the camshaft. In thousands of magazine articles and bench racing sessions, this part has been cussed and discussed, probably to the point of raising more questions and creating more speculation.

To shed some light on the subject, and dispell all those speculative theories, we turned to John Reed of Reed Cams, Peachtree Airport, Chamblee, Georgia. John is one of the brightest men in the business of designing cams for high performance oval track and road racing applications. And he is particularly articulate in explaining his engineering knowledge in a way that would make anyone a camshaft expert.

To understand a camshaft, we must first understand the basic terms associated with it, and also understand what the cam is doing to the valves in their relationship to where the piston is.

The three major terms associated with the camshaft, in their order of importance, are duration, lobe center and lift and acceleration. What these terms are describing is how the cam lifts the valves higher, opens them quicker and holds them open for a period of time. These three items must be very carefully combined according to the application of the engine. The track size, the RPM range the engine is operating in, total vehicle weight, and the engine's volumetric efficiency or breathing capacity are just some of the important considerations when selecting the correct cam for the job.

THE TIMING OF THE EVENTS

You probably know how the four-cycle, internal combustion engine works. It sucks in an air/fuel mixture on the INTAKE stroke, pushes it into a tightly squeezed mass on the COMPRESSION stroke, ignites it on the POWER stroke and scavenges (pushes out) the burned gases on the EXHAUST stroke.

Timing of these events is expressed in degrees of crankshaft rotation. Each stroke takes 180 degrees of crankshaft rotation, for a total of 720 degrees of rotation for the four cycles to occur. The camshaft is directly related to the crankshaft in a 1:2 ratio so the cam rotates at one half of the crankshaft speed. In other words, one cam revolution takes place during two crankshaft revolutions.

CAMSHAFT / KIT ORDER FORM

Reed Engineering Company's application consultants will use this information to determine the best possible camshaft for your use ... so please fill in as completely and as accurately as possible.

NAME: _____

ADDRESS: _____

CITY/STATE: _____

Information to be used as: ☐ Firm Order --- ☐ Recommendation Only

ENGINE:　MAKE OF ENGINE: _____

BLOCK:　ORIGINAL CUBIC INCHES _____ YEAR _____ PRESENT CUBIC INCHES _____

BORE NOW _____ STROKE NOW _____ ORIGINAL TYPE OF LIFTERS _____

VALVES:　HEAD DIAMETER - INTAKE _____ / HEAD DIAMETER - EXHAUST _____

STEM DIAMETER - INTAKE _____ / STEM DIAMETER - EXHAUST _____

　　**NOTE: Are these dimensions same as stock? _____

ASPIRATION:　CARBURETOR MAKE _____ CFM *or* VENTURI AREA _____

NUMBER OF CARB'S ___ JET SIZES: PRIMARIES(____)SECONDARIES(____)

INJECTOR MAKE _____ SUPERCHARGER TYPE _____

ROCKER ARMS:　STOCK? _____ RATIO _____ YEAR _____ TYPE _____

　　　　ADJUSTABLE ( ) OR NON-ADJUSTABLE ( )

CYLINDER HEADS:　PORTED AND POLISHED? _____ AMOUNT MILLED _____

PRESENT CC READING _____ YEAR AND TYPE _____

PISTONS:　MAKE _____ ADVERTISED COMPRESSION RATIO _____

FLAT TOP? _____ HIGH DOME? _____ VALVE POCKETS? (YES) (NO)

If pistons have been fly-cut for extra valve clearance ....
　　HOW MUCH? _____ *INTAKE* _____ *EXHAUST*

CHASSIS:　CAR WEIGHT _____ YEAR/MAKE _____

USE OR CLASS OF COMPETITION _____

(IF BOAT ... WEIGHT, HULL TYPE, DRIVE TYPE _____)

REAR-END GEAR RATIO _____ TRANSMISSION TYPE _____

FLY-WHEEL WEIGHT _____ TIRE DIAMETER _____/SIZE _____

IS CAR STRICTLY TRAILERED? _____

GENERAL INFORMATION:　CAM MAKE, MODEL, TYPE NOW USED _____

I NEED MORE: TOP-END _____ MID-RANGE _____ LOW-END TORQUE _____

BEST SPEED TO DATE _____ BEST E.T. TO DATE _____

BEST OVAL TRACK TIME AND TRACK LENGTH _____

DESIRED RPM TORQUE RANGE: FROM _____ TO _____

DO YOU WISH: HYDRAULIC ☐ SOLID LIFTER ☐ ROLLER TAPPET ☐

COMPLETE ENGINEERED KIT ☐ ASSORTED COMPONENTS ☐ _____

This camshaft order form from Reed Cams gives you an idea of the type of information you should have ready when you order a cam.

The shape and placement of the camshaft lobe determines when the valves are opened and closed, the amount of time in crankshaft degrees they remain open (which is duration) and a how far off the seat they open (lift).

To see how and why each of these events should take place in a high performance engine, let's examine each cycle of the engine closely.

THE INTAKE OPENING

A good rule of thumb in camshaft design and selection is that any change you make in the intake valve timing of an engine via the camshaft has a much more radical change on an engine's torque curve than a change in the exhaust timing events.

Normal logic would say that the intake valve should open when the piston reaches TDC (top dead center) to begin its trip downward, sucking in a fuel/air charge. But this is not the case. To simplify the explanation, the air/fuel charge is lazy in getting its start into the cylinder (it has a low initial velocity), and the valve must be given time to get open all the way, also. Another factor here is the exhaust is still open and gases are rushing out of the cylinder with inertia. This helps "pull" the incoming air/fuel mixture into the cylinder even though the piston is coming up. So in any engine, even a mild street engine, the intake valve is opened before the piston reaches TDC (this is while the piston is still coming up on its last part of the exhaust stroke). This is called the intake side of the total everlap period.

Early intake opening would make you think the incoming air/fuel charge is going to "run out the door" (because the exhaust valve is still open). But this is not how it works. First, there is a little bit of a scavenging action going on. That is, the incoming air/fuel charge helps push the rest of the burnt exhaust gas out through the exhaust valve opening. The great benefit of early intake opening is to allow the engine to breathe longer and receive more air and fuel into the cylinder. If the engine were running at lower speeds (like a street engine staying mostly under 3000 RPM), the result would be a rough idle and very bulky response because the incoming air/fuel would be diluting with the exhaust gas. This is because manifold vacuum is pulling the exhaust back into the incoming air/fuel charge. But at higher engine speeds (we are talking about a racing engine operating anywhere from 3300 to 7200 RPM), the piston has a greater velocity and the incoming air/fuel charge has a greater inertia, meaning there is no manifold vacuum existing, and we are now using this early intake opening to a great advantage. And the higher the engine operating range, the earlier the intake valve can be opened.

THE EXHAUST CLOSES

The intake opening early, combined with the exhaust closing late, constitutes the overlap period. After the piston has reached and passed TDC of the overlap period (which means the exhaust cycle has ceased and the intake cycle has begun), the exhaust valve is still left open. This is done to help draw the incoming air/fuel charge in faster, and it works especially well when the engine has a tuned exhaust system (headers and ported cylinder heads). This is because of an occurance known in fluid hydraulics as "column inertia". As the exhaust gases are pushed out quickly (mostly by combustion pressure rather than the piston), they leave behind a momentary vacuum (the cylinder pressure is below atmospheric pressure). Thus the incoming charge follows in the draft of the outgoing charge. And just as the new charge gets to the exit door of the cylinder, the exhaust valve is shut (if the cam grinder has timed everything right for the RPM range the engine is operating in).

One by-product of this late exhaust valve closing is a slight cooling of the exhaust valve. It has been exposed to extremely hot exhaust gases (at least 1300 degrees). The incoming charge maybe is 100 degrees at the most. So as the new charge reaches the exhaust valve, it cools the valve slightly, preventing excessive heat build-up. It is estimated that without this cooling factor of the overlap period, exhaust valve life would be cut to approximately 10% of its present life.

THE INTAKE CLOSES

This is the timing that really counts. What everything is all about in the four cycles is trying to get as much air/fuel charge into the cylinder as possible before the compression cycle starts. The more air/fuel that is in the cylinder when the spark plug fires, the more powerful the explosion will be (just like the more dynamite you use, the more powerful the explosion you will have). Everything is timed so the cylinder will have every opportunity to fill up.

The intake valve is closed after the piston has reached BDC (bottom dead center). Theoretically, as soon as the piston has reached BDC the compression stroke has begun and if there are any leaks in the cylinder, the piston will push the charge right out that leak (this is called reverse pumping). But because of the long arc of the crankshaft swinging the connecting rod from one side to the other, the piston is actually stalled for a while at BDC, then it takes a little while for the piston velocity to build up again. So the cam grinder takes advantage of this "inactivity" of the piston stroke to let the intake valve stay open and continue filling the cylinder. The built up column inertia of the intake charge will continue filling the cylinder with the piston **well past** BDC and coming up at low speed, overriding the piston movement, to a point.

Extremely late intake closing makes the bottom end of the engine RPM range "bog" and seem unresponsive. The later the intake closing, the higher the RPM range the engine is meant to operate at. For example, on a superspeedway engine, the intake might be closed at 84 degrees ABDC. This puts the engine's torque range between 4000 and 7500 RPM. On a short track engine, you would want to close the intake somewhere around 70 degrees ABDC, pulling the torque range down to 3100 RPM. Of course, there are other considerations in this torque operating range which we will get to shortly.

THE EXHAUST OPENS

Once the intake valve has been closed, the piston swings upward on its compression cycle compacting the air/fuel mixture contained in the cylinder to 1/12th of its original volume (if the compression ratio is 12 to 1). Just before the piston reaches TDC the spark plug fires (at 38 degrees BTDC if this is the advance curve the engine has been given). Giving the spark time to reach and ignite the entire compressed mixture, the piston has reached TDC and the explosion expands the compressed air/fuel charge. This for-ces the piston downward on its power stroke.

The power stroke is only as long as the exhaust valve stays shut. Retarding the exhaust valve opening creates a longer power stroke, which increases bottom end torque. The explosion, though, has usually imparted most of its power through the piston to the crankshaft before the piston has reached a point of travel half way down to the bottom. Once the piston has reached this halfway point in the power stroke, its velocity is diminishing. So nothing is going to be hurt too much if the exhaust valve is opened before the piston reaches BDC. In fact, it will help some because opening the exhaust valve will begin to relieve some of the tremendous pressure which has built up, and allow additional time for the exhaust stroke to complete its function of scavenging the cylinder. Also, the hot exhaust gases can escape the cylinder through the propellant of their own pressure, reducing the need for the engine itself having to expend power on the exhaust stroke forcing them out.

The function of the exhaust valve opening timing has the least effect upon the engine's torque curve than all the other three functions. Changes in timing here are a little more subtle than any of the other three events.

DURATION GUIDELINES

Track Surface	Track Size	Car Weight	Duration*
Dirt	1/4-mile	3000 lbs.	284°-286°
Dirt	1/3, 3/8-mile	3000 lbs.	286°-292°
Dirt	1/2-mile	3000 lbs.	292°-304°
Asphalt	1/4-mile	3000 lbs.	288°-292°
Asphalt	1/3, 3/8-mile	3000 lbs.	298°-304°
Asphalt	1/2-mile	3000 lbs.	308°-310°
Dirt	1/4-mile	3800 lbs.	280°-282°
Dirt	1/3, 3/8-mile	3800 lbs.	282°-288°
Dirt	1/2-mile	3800 lbs.	288°-300°
Asphalt	1/4-mile	3800 lbs.	284°-288°
Asphalt	1/3, 3/8-mile	3800 lbs.	294°-300°
Asphalt	1/2-mile	3800 lbs.	304°-308°
Asphalt	1, 1½-mile	3800 lbs.	310°-314°
Asphalt	2, 2½-mile	3800 lbs.	316°-318°

* Duration measured at .020" tappet height.

DURATION

We have been discussing through all of the valve timing functions how long the valves are staying open. This is their duration.

The definition of duration is "the time in crankshaft degrees of rotation during which the valve is off its seat." In our example cam (timing specification card shown in illustration), the intake duration is 296°. This is computed by adding the intake opening point (42°) to the intake closing point (74°) plus 180°. This equals 296°. Exhaust duration is computed in a similar manner.

When the intake and exhaust lobes of the camshaft are identical in both duration and lift, the cam is called "single pattern." When the exhaust has more duration and lift than the intake, the camshaft is called "dual pattern."

A dual pattern cam of this type stretches the torque range higher in RPMs at the sacrifice of some low RPM torque. Dual pattern cams are used where a wide torque range is required (for example at the Riverside road course where several tight, low speed turns keep the RPMs low, then the mile-long backstretch takes the RPMs up to 7200). Usually, however, more torque can be developed in a shorter RPM range, so this is why you do not see a dual pattern cam in use all the time.

Duration is strictly a function of RPM versus torque. A cam designer selects the duration to achieve the most torque in the range where the engine will be operating. A short duration cam has more torque at a lower RPM range for two reasons: 1) the engine builds up more cylinder pressure on the longer compression stroke, and 2) there is also a longer power stroke as discussed earlier. Duration will not vary between engines, as some other cam specifications will, but only by application. If you have a 3800-pound car which will be running on a flat quarter-mile dirt track, the application will call for a 280° duration (measured at .020" tappet height) whether you have a 351 Ford or a 427 Chevy.

Running duration is the one specification which is not easily compared between manufacturers. This is because each manufacturer rates his cam differently. Let us explain.

First, remember the definition of running duration: "the time in crankshaft degrees of rotation during which the valve is off the seat." This is the only time period which allows the ports to pass air in and out of the cylinder. To measure or rate the cam's duration, then, we must find the point of actual rocker contact with the valve stem on the opening side of the lobe and the actual point of release of the valve stem on the closing side of the lobe. These two figures are then added together to a constant 180° for the actual running duration of the camshaft. For example: the intake rocker opens by contacting the valve stem at 44° before-top-dead-center. Then the piston travels down to bottom-dead-center (180° of movement) and releases the valve stem at 76° after-bottom-dead-center. 44° plus 76° plus 180° equals 300°, so the duration of the camshaft is therefore 300°.

The confusing and controversial problem of rating a cam's duration is merely reduced to finding these opening and closing points accurately. Reed Cams utilizes a constant .020" lifter height for rating camshaft durations. This is the actual point of valve movement off of and back onto its seat again, for accurate and consistant duration ratings. This .020" lifter height measurement is a point **above** the clearance ramp area of the cam lobe which should not be considered as part of duration, since while the lifter is on the clearance ramp the valve is not off its seat. (The clearance ramp is designed onto the lobe to take up the valve lash gradually before the valve is accelerated.)

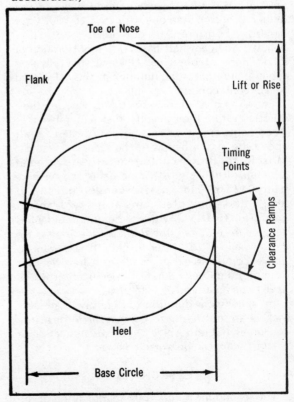

Typical camshaft terms.

Our 300° duration example cam discussed earlier is rated at .020" lifter height. If this same cam was rated at .015"lifter height (an error because the lifter is on the ramp and no valve movement has occurred), the duration would be called 310°. Even though the cam would physically measure 310° at .015" tappet height, the duration rating would be 10° too large, because the point of measurement was wrong.

An excellent "rule of thumb" for finding the running duration is to divide the manufacturer's recommended valve lash by the rocker arm ratio (example: .024 ÷ 1.5 = .016"), and then add .004" for valve train compressability (example: .016" + .004" = .020"). The contact and actual valve movement point is, therefore, .020" lifter height. Compare this figure with the manufacturers stated duration rating point or lifter height. They **should** be the same figure.

A word needs to be added here about the common practice of manufacturers giving .050" lifter height duration figures. This is a very good idea, as it gives the consumer an excellent insight into the rate of valve movement on the camshaft he is buying. Obviously a cam with a duration of 265° at .050" lifter height is a much larger and higher RPM cam than one with 255° at .050" lifter height, if both are 300° duration at .020" lifter height. Any camshaft has a different duration at all different lifter heights. However, the only true running duration is the duration at the calculated rocker contact point.

For examples of manufacturers varying their duration rating lifter heights, first remember that Reed cams are rated at a height of .020", well above the actual height of the clearance ramp. Most Racer Brown cams generally are rated at a height of .017", most Crane cams at anywhere from .012" to .018", most Iskenderian cams at .012", and Chevrolet cams at many different heights up to .015". With the duration guidelines we give in the table, the duration specified is for cams rated at .020" lifter height. If you want to find a comparable cam made by Chevrolet, for example, the Chevy duration specification would have to be measured at .020" also.

In specifying duration differently, camshaft makers are not trying to confuse or mislead the consumer, but rather give him a true indication of what the cam can be expected to do.

LOBE CENTER

The second most important specification of the camshaft is its lobe center. Lobe center is the angle between the geometric centerline of the intake lobe and the geometric centerline of the exhaust lobe. This is a fixed position which cannot be altered once the cam has been ground.

Lobe center sometimes is confused with lobe centerline. The centerline refers to the angle between the lobe center and the crankshaft TDC. Lobe centerline is what is changed when the cam is advanced or retarded (which we will discuss shortly).

The most normal lobe center angle on a racing engine camshaft is 108 degrees. When the lobe center angle is shortened (for example to 106 degrees), the low range torque of the engine will pick up. Increasing the center angle (for example to 110 degrees) gains torque in the higher RPMs. The closer center angle allows the cylinder to build up more cylinder pressure because the intake valve is closed earlier. More cylinder pressure directly equals more lower end torque. The lobe center is carefully chosen by the cam grinder to open and close the valves exactly when it is correct for the RPM range in which the engine will operate.

OVERLAP

Overlap is not a figure which is chosen and ground into a camshaft, but rather overlap falls into place on the cam as a by-product of duration and lobe center. The shorter the lobe center angle, the longer the overlap period. And consequently, the longer the duration, the longer the overlap.

A formula which is used to determine the overlap on single pattern cams is "duration minus two times the lobe center angle equals the overlap." In algebraic terms this would be expressed:

$$d - 2l = o$$

where **d** equals duration, **l** equals lobe center angle and **o** equals overlap.

Overlap is the period of time during which the intake and exhaust valves are both open together. The primary functions of doing this are the scavenging (pushing out) of the exhaust gases, and drawing in early the fresh intake charge. At high RPMs, the incoming air/fuel charge has enough velocity to actually help push the exhaust gases out the exhaust port. This will help the cylinder fill up quicker and cleaner. The higher the RPMs of the engine, the better this scavenging action works, so an overlap period of up to 102 degrees can be used on superspeedway engines. For a very short track where RPMs are held low coming off a turn, overlap in the range of 65 to 72 degrees is more in order.

VALVE LIFT

Valve lift is one of the most important factors to consider for engine breathing. The more the valve lifts off its seat the greater the opening there is in the head for gases to flow by.

But when we talk about valve lift, we must also talk about valve acceleration rate. A cylinder is given only a certain allotted time in which to fill up with an incoming charge. So it is far better to lift the valve off its seat rapidly so the gases have a longer period of time in which to flow without any interferences.

The latest technology in camshaft grinding is increasing the lift and acceleration. Lift rate is measured in thousandths of an inch per degree of rotation. What camshaft makers are trying to do is get the valve to lift higher for every degree of rotation. But to do that, the lift figure must also get taller. This is because the cam must have a safety margin built in which decelerates the tappet as the nose of the cam approaches. If it does not slow down, the tappet will fly off and loose its contact with the cam lobe. So the compromise here is either a higher lift with a deceleration ramp at the nose or unbearably high valve spring rates to control acceleration. It is with a high lift, high opening velocity cam that you want to be sure you have a top quality cam. Extreme valve spring tension may cause extreme rubbing pressures of the tappet on the lobe, wearing (or even breaking) the lobe very quickly. This is also the reason a proper lube procedure should be followed while installing the cam.

THE CLEARANCE RAMP

The clearance ramp is a term we have already mentioned, but not really defined. It is an area on the cam which gently raises the lifter off the heel of the cam, taking up the clearance (or lash) in the system. Once everything is hooked up and ready to move, the valve acceleration rate comes in and begins moving the valve at a velocity 20 times greater than what it was moving on the clearance ramp.

There is a danger of the valve lifter by-passing the clearance ramp on the lobe if the valve lash is set with too much clearance. Let's say for example that a cam lobe has a .016" high clearance ramp. This times a 1.5 rocker arm ratio equals .024". This is what the maximum valve lash should be on the intake lobe. But to be safe, every cam maker builds in a safety factor of appoxi-mately .004", so the specification card which comes with the camshaft might say the cam should have .020" lash (.024" minus safety factor of .004").

This builds in some adjustment of valve lash so the mechanic has some leeway for fine tuning. But a recommended valve lash setting should never be exceeded by .002"-.003" in either direction. If this has to be exceeded for best performance, then this is an indication a different camshaft profile is required.

VALVE LASH

Valve lash is a slack, or clearance, in the valve train designed in on purpose to compensate for any thermal expansion of the valve train components as the engine heats up during operation. If no lash was present, the valves would not close all the way in a hot engine.

Tightening or loosening the valve lash from the manufacturer's specification changes the timing slightly of when the cam lobe makes contact with the tappet. A change of .001" in lash can make as much as 3 degrees difference (depending on cam) at the cam in timing. On most modern cams, tightening the valve lash adds top end torque and horsepower. Loosening the lash does just the opposite, or adds bottom end torque (in effect, shortens duration).

When using valve lash as a fine tuning tool, it is far safer to tighten the lash than to loosen it. Most cams can tolerate as much as .008" tighter lash, whereas most cams will not tolerate any more than .002"-.003" looser lash.

Valve lash in a high performance engine must constantly be checked and adjusted to maintain the performance level and prevent valve train damage from inaccurate lash settings. Valve lash must also be maintained constant from cylinder to cylinder for the most power output, and when changing lash, the same amount should be changed on both intake and exhaust.

ADVANCING AND RETARDING

Advancing or retarding the cam position in relationship to the crankshaft is another tuning tool available.

Advancing a cam opens the intake earlier and closes the exhaust earlier, producing more low range torque at the sacrifice of some top end power. Retarding the cam increases mid and top range torque but hurts the bottom end performance.

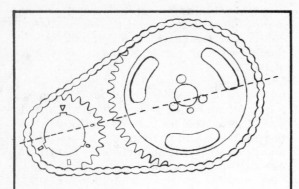

1. **FOR STANDARD TIMING**
   Use Keyway marked "O"
   Time Engine from Sprocket Tooth, or Tooth Space with Timing Mark "O". This is the same as the O.E.M. setting

2. **FOR 4° CAMSHAFT ADVANCE**
   Use Keyway Marked " △ " (Triangle)
   Time Engine from Sprocket tooth or tooth space with Timing Mark " △ "

3. **FOR 4° CAMSHAFT RETARD**
   Use Keyway Marked " ▭ " (Rectangle or Bar)
   Time Engine from Sprocket tooth or tooth space with Timing Mark " ▭ "

   DO NOT USE the Keyway Timing Marks to Time Engine. Always use the Tooth or Tooth Space Timing Marks.

This drawing of a Cloyes timing gear and roller chain set illustrates how it can be adjustable for camshaft timing advance or retard.

Advancing or retarding can be accomplished in two ways, either at the camshaft or the crankshaft. At the cam, it is held in place on the cam gear by use of a dowel. The dowel hole can be drilled larger and an offset bushing can be installed, which moves the cam position in relationship to the cam gear. These offset bushings are available from Mr. Gasket Company and most cam makers.

At the crankshaft, the crank is held in position with the crank timing gear by using a straight key in a keyway slot. This straight key can be replaced by an offset key to change the line-up of the timing gear to the crankshaft. These, as well as the cam offset bushings, are available in all increments from 1 degree to 8 degrees, (remember that 4 degrees at the cam is 8 degrees at the crank).

Advancing the cam will slightly decrease the valve-to-piston clearance of the intake valves. Retarding the cam will bring the exhaust valve closer to the pistons.

ROLLER CAMS

A roller cam is similar to a flat tappet cam except the tappet (or cam follower) contains a roller bearing which rolls over the lobe surface instead of sliding on it.

Using a roller cam has many advantages. In any performance engine, a roller cam allows the use of a more radical cam lobe profile. Valve acceleration rate, velocity and lift can be increased because not nearly as much clearance ramp is required and the design is not bound by the diameter of the flat solid lifter.

At left, round offset bushings and offset keys show the different ways of changing camshaft timing. Center, positive cam retainer button is shown at upper-right with cam retainer plate which has been drilled oversize to accept offset bushing. Drawing at right shows how cam bushing is used to retard cam. Arrow shows direction of engine rotation.

Less running friction is generated with a roller cam, so the engine is not putting out as much of its own energy to overcome this friction. Another benefit of this reduced friction is a cooler oil temperature, and very little cam wear.

The reduction of friction with the roller also enables the engine to free some torque which ordinarily would be used up with the flat tappet cam. This helps the roller cam add additional horsepower.

A roller cam also allows the use of higher spring rate tensions and higher RPM operating ranges.

ROCKER ARM RATIO

The rocker arm ratio is the leverage ratio of the pivot to valve stem seat divided by the pivot to push rod seat leagth.

Because the camshaft lobe height is multiplied by the rocker arm ratio to yield the total lift of the valve off its seat (minus valve lash, of course), it is easy to see that a greater rocker arm ratio will cause a higher lift.

The advantage of using a greater rocker arm ratio is to increase breathing and power on the top end of the engine range. It achieves this by giving the valve a higher lift, and a greater opening and closing acceleration velocity which increases the all important area under the valve lift curve. Rocker arm ratio has little effect on duration or overlap

In cases where it is desired to increase the rocker arm ratio, special rocker arms are available from many sources such as Reed, Crane, Iskenderian, Harlan Sharp, etc. Any replacement rocker arm you use should ride on needle bearings.

The obvious place to use a greater than stock rocker arm ratio is where the torque range must be extended on the top end.

DEGREEING THE CAM

Degreeing the camshaft after its installation is a very simple process, yet one which many engine builders skip because they do not understand the procedure, or why it is done.

The reasons behind camshaft degreeing are very important. To make sure an engine delivers its full maximum power potential, the engine builder must know the camshaft is phased to the crankshaft correctly so valve opening and closing times are correct in relation to piston position.

To degree the cam, three tools are required: a degree wheel, a pointer and a dial indicator. The degree wheel is a round metal or plasic disc marked off in 360 equal degrees, and bolted to the front of the crankshaft. Degree wheels are available from almost every cam maker for only a few dollars.

The pointer is nothing more than a piece of heavy gauge metal wire with a sharpened tip at the end. It is held in place on the engine by a

The pointer is at TDC on the degree wheel after the piston has been synchronized to the wheel. The engine was rotated in each direction from TDC until the dial indicator showed .100 in. of travel down the bore. The degrees [on the wheel] were noted at each .100 in. of travel, and these degrees were averaged to obtain the same amount of piston travel in each direction to obtain TDC.

We're still degreeing the cam, but just using slightly different hardware. The point is, you can use any type of pointer and degree wheel, just so long as you are accurate. Notice the gear drive for the cam.

timing cover bolt usually, and bent to point at the degree markings on the degree wheel.

The dial indicator is clamped in place magneticly on top of the deck and is used to accurately determine when the piston has reached TDC and to determine precisely when the cam lobe starts to lift.

There can be several reasons why the camshaft, as installed seemingly correct, is out of phase with the crankshaft. The dowel pin in the cam may be located incorrectly, the keyway in the crankshaft may be out of place, or the dowel pin hole or keyway hole in the timing gears may be located incorrectly. Just small tolerances being off on one or more of these can cause the cam to be out of phase a couple of degrees.

First, the TDC of the #1 cylinder must be found. The engine can be rotated so the piston is visually at TDC, but even with the steadiest hand, it will still be off by a few degrees. Clamp the dial

The dial indicator measures lift of cam against modified tappet. Care must be taken to be sure the indicator plunger runs in the same axis as the tappet.

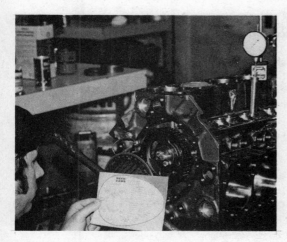

With degree wheel, pointer and dial indicator in place, Wilson consults camshaft specification card which is supplied with cam for degreeing.

indicator down on the deck and set the point straight up and down to the cylinder bore (check this alignment very closely). Rotate the crank back and forth until the dial indicator shows that TDC has been reached.

Now the degree wheel and TDC must be synchronized. With the piston at TDC and the dial

indicator set on zero, rotate the engine until the dial indicator shows .100" travel. Make a note of the degree reading on the wheel (in the case of the engine we degreed, it was 17½ degrees in the clockwise rotation.). Then the engine is rotated the opposite way back up to TDC and continued in the opposite direction until the dial indicator shows .100" of travel. The degree wheel is read again (in the case of our example engine, the degree wheel showed 16¼ degrees).

If the degree wheel reading is not the same in each direction of travel, as is the case in the examples we cited, average the two degree readings and move the wheel on the pointer. In our example, the average is 16 7/8 degrees, so while the dial indicator still showed .100" of travel, the degree wheel was moved opposite the pointer to 16 7/8 degrees.

Once the degree wheel and piston are synchronized on the #1 cylinder, set the degree wheel to zero opposite the pointer with the piston at TDC, and install a tappet on the #1 intake lobe. This tappet should have an extension on it so the dial indicator can make contact with it while clamped on its base on the cylinder deck. Wilson uses a special tappet which has been machined with a long extender on top. The same thing can be

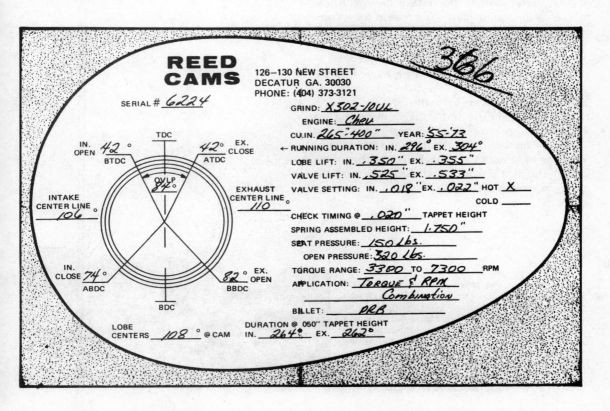

REED CAMS

126–130 NEW STREET
DECATUR GA. 30030
PHONE: (404) 373-3121

366

SERIAL # *6224*

TDC

IN. OPEN *42* °
BTDC

42 ° EX. CLOSE
ATDC

OVLP
84 °

INTAKE CENTER LINE °
106

EXHAUST CENTER LINE °
110

IN. CLOSE *74* °
ABDC

82 ° EX. OPEN
BBDC

BDC

GRIND: *X302-10UL*
ENGINE: *Chev*
CU.IN. *265"-400"*   YEAR: *'55-'73*
← RUNNING DURATION: IN. *296°* EX. *304°*
LOBE LIFT: IN. *.350"* EX. *.355"*
VALVE LIFT: IN. *.525"* EX. *.533"*
VALVE SETTING: IN. *.018"* EX. *.022"* HOT *X*
            COLD _____
CHECK TIMING @ *.020"* TAPPET HEIGHT
SPRING ASSEMBLED HEIGHT: *1.750"*
SEAT PRESSURE: *150 Lbs.*
OPEN PRESSURE: *320 Lbs.*
TORQUE RANGE: *3300* TO *7300* RPM
APPLICATION: *Torque & RPM*
            Combination
BILLET: *PRB*

LOBE CENTERS *108* ° @ CAM
DURATION @ .050" TAPPET HEIGHT
IN. *264°* EX. *262°*

accomplished by welding a bolt on top of an old tappet.

To check the cam timing, move the crankshaft clockwise until the tappet is on the camshaft heel. Position the dial indicator point on the tappet extension and preload the indicator maybe .050", then set the indicator to zero.

At this time consult the timing specification card which was included with the camshaft. It has a checking height specified. For example, on our sample cam, the chacking height is .020" (as it is on all Reed cams, although every cam maker has his own checking height).

Rotate the crankshaft clockwise until the dial indicator shows .020" movement has occured. Then check the degree wheel. The pointer should be pointing at the same number of degrees as the timing card says the intake opens BTDC. In the case of our example cam, the degree wheel should be reading 42 degrees, as the time spec card shows. Record the reading obtained with the cam in the specified BTDC position. Then rotate the crankshaft clockwise again. The indicator will detect the full lift, then descend on the other side of the lobe. As the indicator shows .020" once more, check the degree wheel. The number being pointed at on the degree wheel should correspond to the intake closing ABDC figure on the timing card. The reason for recording these figures is so you can compare them to the timing card later on in case the cam needs to be advanced or retarded.

The extended tappet should be moved to the exhaust lobe of the #1 cylinder and this procedure should be repeated again for the exhaust.

Once the exhaust and intake timing figures have been checked on the cam against the timing card, add up the intake duration and the exhaust duration to be sure they check against the timing card. This is a precaution check to be sure the cam was ground accurately.

If you compare the figures you actually measured with the cam and find the intake opens sooner and closes sooner than the timing card says it should, then the cam is advanced. For example, if the intake should open at 42° BTDC and it actually opened at 44° BTDC, the cam is advanced 2°. A cam retard offset bushing should be used to get the timing back into its intended position (which is called split overlap).

Cam installation and break-in is covered in the engine assembly chapter of this book. A note about cam break-in: If, after the initial break-in run the rocker arms are real loose (large lash clearance), suspect that the lobes on the cam have worn.

The grooves in the lobes of this cam indicate crankshaft failure. This cam only ran 15 minutes on the dyno, with all proper procedures being taken by a professional engine builder. Please note this is a roller cam, not a flat tappet cam and thus the nose profile was already shaped like shown before the cam was installed. The failure here was the grooves in the lobes. However, many times a flat tappet cam will wear   the nose during its break-in run giving it a profile that looks like a roller cam.

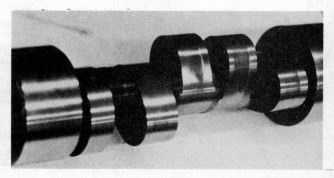

The Valve Train

Selecting the right components and concentrating on some small details in the valve train will assure that your engine will perform to its maximum, free some lost horsepower and rev to its potential.

The most important details in the valve train include selecting the right rocker arms in terms of durability and stiffness-to-weight ratio, selecting the right components to avoid component flexing, and checking for correct geometry.

ROCKER ARMS

When you add a high lift cam and stiffer than stock valve springs, the stock stamped rocker arms are too weak to get the job done. The stock rocker contact balls, also, are not adequate in lubrication capacity to get the job done. Aftermarket rocker arms are required, with the ideal combination being high strength and light weight. The arms should be forged aluminum alloy with needle bearing pivots (trunions) and roller contact fulcrums (for the Chevy 350 and Ford 351-C). For the Chrysler 340, which employs shaft mounted rockers, use the Chrysler part numbers P3870718 and P3870719 (intakes), and P3870720 (exhausts). This is a forged steel adjustable rocker, with a 1.5:1 ratio. Be sure to stay away from ductile iron rocker arms for the 340—they have a history of breakage during high RPM usage. For the rocker arm shaft, use Chrysler part number P3870728.

The rocker arms which Wilson uses for the Chevy 350 is the Crane extruded aluminum part number 11757 (for 1.6:1 ratio) or Crane number 11756 (for 1.5:1 ratio). In the Ford 351-C, he uses the Crane part number 27750 (which is a stock 1.73:1 ratio). The Crane rockers have shown themselves to wear well in thousands of miles of super speedway racing in comparison to other brands of arms, and this is the real test of valve train components. The Crane arms feature needle bearing trunions and roller fulcrums. These features lower the operating temperature of the components by lowering friction and wear. Needle bearings and roller fulcrums can operate under marginal lubrication conditions (such as when high G forces momentarily push oil away from the rocker arms) without failure, whereas the stock type of arms cannot endure this.

The MoPar 340 valve train with the Chrysler "P" part forged steel rockers.

Whenever you get a set of these high performance rocker arms, do not try to lighten them or polish them. They have been designed to withstand the stresses they will encounter, and any material removal will only serve to weaken them, defeating your purpose. While lightness is a good quality in the valve train, stiffness is more important to make sure nothing flexes.

A periodic maintenance check of the rocker arms is a good idea in order to spot any trouble. If you discover any scuffing or galling of the roller tip, the rocker arm tip, or valve stem tip scuffing, then start checking for rocker arm geometry problems.

ROCKER ARM RATIO

The rocker arm ratio is the difference between the lift as measured at the valve and the lift measured at the camshaft lobe. The reason for the difference lies in the fact that the rocker arm is longer on one side of its pivot than it is on the other, resulting in a leverage ratio which multiplies the movement from the cam lobe to the valve. For example, if an arm has a length of 1" from the pushrod to the pivot center, and 1½" from the pivot center to the valve stem contact, then the ratio is 1.5:1. The stock ratio for the Chevy 350 and Chrysler 340 is 1.5:1, while the Ford 351-C is designed at 1.73:1. Generally in competition engines, the Chevy and Chrysler ratios are increased while the Ford ratio is never increased.

This rocker arm ratio we have defined is a theoretical ratio. In actual practice, the ratio will be somewhat lower because of valve train deflection, although if you have chosen the correct

pieces, this deflection will be minimal. Manufacturing tolerances on all the valve train components can also change the rocker arm ratio somewhat.

Increasing the rocker arm ratio will definitely increase the valve lift and other cam specifications, making it a desirable change. But consider this: the rocker arm ratio times the pounds-per-inch of valve spring open pressure equals the net load being applied against the cam, so it is possible to overload the cam lobe by indiscriminately changing the rocker arm ratio. Be sure you tell the camshaft maker which rocker arm ratio you will be using when you order a cam. It can make a difference. If the valve spring open pressure exceeds the recommendations of the cam grinder, severe lobe wear can result.

ROCKER ARM GEOMETRY

Rocker arm geometry is basically a very simple concept, but many times overlooked. What it deals with is the relationship between the rocker arm contact point and the valve stem tip. Because the rocker arm moves in a semi-circular rocking path and the valve stem moves straight up and down, naturally the relationship and the leverage ratio between the two will always be changing. What ideal rocker arm geometry implies is that the arm contact radius is in the center of the valve stem tip at exactly half of the valve lift.

Correct rocker arm geometry minimizes side loads on the valve stems, which lengthens the wear life of the valve stem, the valve guide and the rocker arm, and also gains some free horsepower for the engine by relieving some friction.

There are a number of factors which can change

the rocker arm geometry: pushrod length, cylinder head and block milling, rocker arm ratio, and miscellaneous component manufacturing tolerances. They can all add up to affect the ideal geometry.

You can and should check the geometry of your valve train. To do this, bolt a cylinder head with the number one intake and exhaust valves installed intact onto the block (be sure to use a head gasket and torque the bolts to specification). Only the outer valve springs need to be installed. Set a dial indicator on the head with the indicator point preloaded on the valve spring retainer. Rotate the camshaft until the indicator shows you have found maximum lift of the cam. From maximum lift, rotate the camshaft exactly 180 degrees, which will put the lifter on the center of the heel of the cam, and then zero the dial indicator. Rotate the cam until half of the total valve lift is reached, then inspect the relationship between the rocker arm fulcrum radius and the valve stem tip. At this point it should be exactly in the middle of the valve stem tip. If it is inside of the center of the valve stem tip (toward the camshaft), the pushrod is too short. If the rocker arm fulcrum contacts the valve stem tip outside of the center of it, the pushrod is too long. On the shaft mounted Chrysler rocker arms, instead of the pushrod being too long, the rocker stands are high. The converse is also true. In the case of the Chrysler, if the stands must be higher, shim material must be machined and installed. If the stand must be lower, they must be milled. In the case of Fords and Chevrolets, longer and shorter length pushrods are available from Crane Cams.

This same rocker arm geometry process can also be used to check if all the rocker arms in the set yield the same valve lift. Install all of the arms of the set, one at a time, on the same cylinder and use the dial indicator on the valve spring retainer to follow the arm through maximum valve lift. Use a degree wheel and pointer to know where the camshaft is. Rotate the camshaft from the center of its heel to maximum lift on each rocker arm, recording the lift the dial indicator shows for each arm. The maximum lift should not vary among the entire set of arms by more than .005", although you'll find it hard to find this close a tolerance.

PUSHRODS

Just like all valve train components, the pushrods have to have a maximum stiffness with a minimum of weight. The best aftermarket type of pushrod to use is a tubular rod, which has the greatest stiffness to weight ratio. But, don't overlook the stock parts first. Wilson has found them to be suited for the job in super speedway racing engines, and their cost is definitely lower. The factory part numbers are 3796243 for the Chevy 350, P3690988 for the Chrysler 340, and M-6565-A342 for the Cleveland Ford.

This photo illustrates the all important relationship of rocker arm roller to valve stem tip, with the valve seated. Notice how far forward on the valve stem tip the rocker already is. As the valve is lifted off its seat, the roller will move forward, which will put this roller way to the outer edge of the stem tip. This is improper rocker arm geometry, and will cause extreme outer edge valve stem tip wear. When the valve is seated, the rocker should properly rest at the inside edge of the tip, with the roller centered on the tip at half lift.

Factory stock pushrods are not manufactured under the best of quality control conditions, so be sure to check every new pushrod for straightness. To do that, roll them on a flat surface.

Every time you have the heads off your racing engine, check the pushrods for straightness, and check the tips for galling. You could catch a problem before it becomes major with this check as part of your regular routine maintenance.

VALVE SPRINGS

While the cam is important for opening the valves, the correct valve spring is vitally important for the precision timing of the valve closing. The valve spring is a significant factor for efficient engine operation.

The valve spring tension must just be stiff enough to allow the lifter to follow the contour of the cam. If the spring is too light in its tension, valve float can result. If it is too stiff, accelerated valve train component wear is just around the corner.

Valve float is one of the most dreaded problems in the valve train. The problem occurs when the valve spring tension is not great enough to allow the lifter to follow the cam lobe. The valve spring may be too weak at the outset, or it may have fatigued from wear and lost its specified tension. In either case, the valve will hang open, then snap closed. This action can destroy valve seats, break the valve head off the stem, break the retainer, bend pushrods, or cause piston-to-valve contact. Any of these possibilities can destroy your engine, so it makes sense to give special attention to the

The valve springs Wilson uses are custom made for him by Precision Spring. The retainer is by Manley. At right is a TRW spring shim used to correct valve spring tension. At bottom is a Perfect Circle teflon valve stem oil seal.

valve springs.

Valve spring surge is another problem you may encounter when stiffer valve springs are coupled with high operating RPMs. This can also result in valve float. Surge is the vibration created by the natural frequency of the spring being excited. Because of this fact, an opposing spring load and/or a damper is required to combat surge. An opposing spring is an inner spring which is wound at an angle opposite the direction of the outside spring. In many cases, the inner spring has an interference fit with the outer spring, creating a damping effect. In other cases, a damper made of coiled flat steel is inserted between the inner and outer springs to control surge.

Most important to the life of a racing valve spring is the material from which it is constructed. Some springs are made from high quality alloys such as vanadium chrome steel or silicone chrome steel, but the best material by far is a new alloy known as Vasco. It retains its original tension much longer than any other alloy.

Which brand of valve springs should you use? The best recommendation we can make is to purchase the entire cam kit from the cam manufacturer. The complete kit would include the cam, inner and outer valve springs, retainers and keepers. This helps you eliminate a lot of guesswork. The cam manufacturer has undoubtedly carried out a lot of research to determine what springs are required and what spring tensions his cam can withstand.

INSTALLING VALVE SPRINGS

The first thing to consider is that racing valve springs vary in size from the stock springs most heads are designed to accommodate, enough so that some metal removal will be required to fit most springs. We won't give any dimensions for particular heads here, because different brand springs can require different machining dimensions.

To machine the valve guides to accept the inner and outer springs, a counterboring tool must be used to narrow the valve guides and widen the spring seats. This operation can be done by most engine machine shops, or you can do it yourself with a tool rented from one of several camshaft manufacturers. Any racing valve springs you purchase will come with an instruction sheet showing the dimensional changes required to accommodate the particular springs. On most heads, the valve spring seats are very close to the water jackets, so be extremely careful when machining the valve spring seats.

MEASURING SPRING TENSION

There are three specifications for all valve springs: assembled height, seat pressure and open pressure. All three of these will be specified by the cam grinder on his specification card, and these should be closely adhered to. He has the engineering expertise to determine what tension is required to make the tappet follow the lobe, as well as determining the maximum pressure his cam will be able to endure.

The assembled height is the checking height to which the spring assembly is compressed when determining the seat pressure on a valve spring rate checker. The seat pressure is the tension which the spring places against the valve when it is seated in the head. The open pressure is the tension the spring exerts when it is compressed by the cam lobe forcing the rocker arm down on the spring.

Of the two pressure specifications, the seat pressure is more critical than open pressure. This is because if there is not enough seat pressure, the valve will not close properly. Too weak a seat pressure can also allow the valve to bounce on the seat.

To check the head assembly for correct installed height of the spring, insert a valve into a guide, and install the spring retainer and keepers on the valve stem. Pull the valve up by the retainer as tight as you can, then measure with a snap gauge or inside micrometer the distance from the spring seat to the retainer. This should be the installed height as specified by the camshaft manufacturer. If the distance is greater than the specified height, shims must be added on the spring seat to close the gap. Once the installed height is determined with shims, place the springs on the spring rate checker base, put the spring and the spring retainer on the shims, then compress the spring to the installed height. Observe the spring rate. Then compress the spring the amount of the valve lift. The spring pressure gauge should show the open pressure specified for the spring. In reality, all the spring assemblies will not work out to be the same. The allowable tolerance should be to have the springs all within 5 pounds per inch of each other. It may be necessary to juggle inner and outer springs around in order to achieve the tolerance in all springs.

For an example of how the spring rate check works, let's say the assembled height of a spring assembly should be 1.750". Compress the spring to this on the inch scale for the seat pressure reading. If the valve lift of the cam is .525", subtract this from 1.750" and compress the spring to 1.225" to check the open pressure.

When checking the open pressure, use a feeler gauge to determine if there is at least .010" clearance between each coil of the spring. There

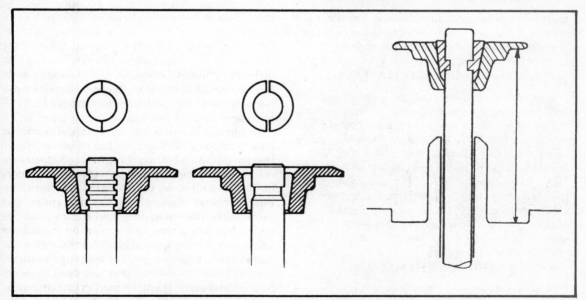

In the two illustrations at left, the wrong and the right way to install keepers is shown. The keepers should have at least .010" distance between them, like the right one, rather than butt together as the left one shows. If they butt together, they can allow the retainer to loosen. At right, the assembled height of a valve spring is shown.

The spring retainers and keepers have been measured on the finished valve in the head with a snap gauge. Then the valve springs are placed in a spring tester and compressed to the installed height. At that height the spring pressure is checked, to be compared against all other springs in order to keep all springs uniform.

must be in order to avoid coil bind. Do not fully compress the spring when checking its open rate. This can overstress and weaken the spring.

RETAINER TO GUIDE CLEARANCE

When a greater than stock valve lift is used, the rocker arm travels downward further than in stock engines. Because of this there is a good possibility the spring retainer may contact the valve guide when the valve is at full lift. Check this before assembling the heads. If there is not at least 1/8" clearance between the retainer and valve guide, the guide must be shortened. Do not shorten the guide any more than is absolutely necessary to obtain the 1/8" clearance, as the guide is what stabilizes the valve.

THE VALVE STEM SEAL

A good valve stem seal is important to prevent oil from draining into the ports from the rocker arm area. As you know, oil consumption kills horsepower. The best type of seal to use is the Perfect Circle teflon type which clamps to the top

of the guide. Perfect Circle makes a tool which can be used to machine the top of the guide to accept their seal.

VALVE TO PISTON CLEARANCE

You may have been going along fine for many races, with no problems of valve to piston clearance. Then all of a sudden you make one component change, and your valves contact the pistons creating instant junk. The component change can be one of many things: crank stroke, longer rod length, different piston top configuration, different size valves, or larger camshaft lift or longer duration. And even if a component manufacturer guarantees you will not have any clearance problems, you can only be sure if you check it yourself.

The period during which valve to piston contact is most likely to occur is near the end of the exhaust stroke and the start of the intake stroke. This is because the cam may be accelerating the valves quicker than the piston is moving. Because of this and the possibilities of thermal expansion, it is recommended that a minimum of .080" on the intake and .100" on the exhaust clearance be kept between the valve at its maximum lift and the piston at its highest point of travel. The exhaust gets a greater tolerance because the cam retards itself to a certain degree at high RPMs.

There are several methods of checking piston to valve clearance, but only one can really be recommended here. That method is the clay method. Other measuring methods are carried out with the piston in only one specific position, while the clay method accurately measures the clearance without any specific regard to piston and valve positions (because the method automatically takes all positions into consideration).

To check the clearance, lay a strip of modeling clay (at least 3/16" thick) on top of one piston in the partially assembled engine so that it completely covers both valve pockets. Lay a clean, used head gasket on the block, attach the cylinder head and torque it to specification. The tappets, pushrods and rocker arms should be added for the cylinder being checked. Adjust the valve lash to hot specifications, then rotate the crankshaft through two complete revolutions. This will allow both the intake and exhaust valves to open and close. If you encounter any resistance in the engine while trying to rotate the crankshaft, stop and investigate. It may be that you are feeling valve-to-piston contact. In most engines, it is possible to look through either the spark plug

The heads are fitted with outer valve springs only for initial engine break-in on dyno. Springs are by Precision Spring. The retainers and keepers are by Manley. Notice gap in keeper halves, and threaded studs for Jomar spacer and valve covers.

hole or the exhaust port with an inspection light in order to see what the obstruction is.

After rotating the crank, carefully disassemble the head. If the valves have not made an impression in the clay, you are in good shape. If the valves have made an impression, cut the clay in half with a very sharp knife and measure its thickness at its thinnest point with a micrometer or machinists' scale.

If there is not the minimum clearance we specified, the pistons will have to be fly-cut. Be careful though when notching pistons. It is possible to get the piston tops too thin. The piston should maintain a top thickness of at least .200". The fly cutting should be done by an experienced machine shop, as it is easy to ruin a set of expensive pistons. Also, be sure to tell the machinist which piston belongs to which cylinder. Remember that some pistons will have an exhaust valve on the left, whereas it will be located on the right side on others.

THE VALVE JOB

The proper valve face angle has two important purposes: helping to flow as much gas as possible, and helping to cool the valves. Valve heads are cooled principally by their contact with the seats where the heat is transferred into the cylinder head.

The valve angles to use with the seat angles specified by Cylinder Heads America in the cylinder head chapter elsewhere in this book are a 45° seat (.100" wide) with a 30° top cut above the seat. These angles, which apply to both the intake and exhaust, have been determined by CHA to be superior for both flow and cooling.

WHICH VALVES

There is enough to be said about the durability and flow characteristics of different valves to fill up one complete book. For our discussion here, we will specify which valves have been determined to be best on both counts after countless hours of research plus actual on-the-track testing.

For the 350 Chevrolet, use the Chevy 366285 (2.05-inch diameter) intake and TRW S2699H exhaust. In the MoPar 340, use Chrysler part number P3690230 intake and P3690231 exhaust. In the Ford 351-C, two different combinations have been found to work well—either Manley or Ford valves. The Manley part numbers are 11810 for the intake and 11811 for the exhaust. For the Ford parts, use number M-6507-D321 intake valve and M-6505-D321 exhaust.

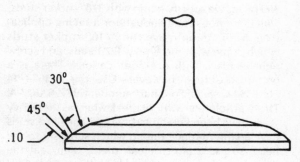

30°

45°

.10

Valve-Seat Face

The Jomar rocker stud girdle in place on a Chevy 350. This is a mandatory part on the Chevy to stabilize the valve train.

An assembly note for valves: coat the stems of the valves with a half and half mixture of STP and oil just before slipping them into the heads.

JOMAR STUD GIRDLE

A Jomar stud girdle should be utilized to keep the valve train assembly protected and rigid from the high rev vibrations which are encountered by the valve train in a racing engine. Rocker arm stud flex can reduce valve lift and duration by as much as .025'' and 10°. Stud flex will also retard the effective valve opening significantly. The stud girdle should definitely be used on the Chevy 350, Chevy 427, and AMC 360 and 390 engines. It is also available for the Ford 351-C, but experience has shown it is not necessary in this engine.

A note about studs is in order here. The Chevy 350 heads we specify come with 3/8'' rocker studs, which are not strong enough for a racing application. Many people use the 7/16'' rocker studs which come with the Chevy 427 heads, and screw right in place with no modifications. There is a better substitute, however. Use the 7/16''—14 Ford 351-C studs, Ford part number C9ZZ-6A527-A. These absolutely will not break whereas the Chevy studs have been known to give up. The Ford studs have an interference thread which screws into the head, so use a tap to clean them, then seal the threads with Loctite when installing. The Ford studs also have more threads for the adjusting screws.

Cylinder Heads

Throughout this book we have presented information which will allow you to build a competitive and **durable** engine. Of course, performing all of the modifications outlined will also help the engine produce more horespower over the stock version. But now we will let you in on where the real horsepower is achieved in an engine: cylinder head port development.

In its original configuration, a cylinder head port is not designed for best performance. Some engines have better port design than others, but optimum flow is not a criteria when engineers design an engine.

Porting, basically, is the science of establishing a controlled flow pattern into and out of the combustion chamber. And, this overall pattern is established with a judicious and well-tested choice of port cross-sectional dimensions, shaping and surface finish.

Cylinder head port modification is an exacting science, yet there are no formulas or hard and fast rules which hold true for all engines and port configurations. Small changes, seemingly unimportant ones, can make important changes in flow. So, the only way to really know what effect any changes in the ports will make is to test the head on a flow bench. It might be important to note here, before we delve into it further, that there are many different means to accomplish the same end in port development, with different porting shops subscribing to different methods. But the only true test of a cylinder head modification is if it works on the engine.

THE VALVE SEATS

Because the valve is the single biggest restriction to port breathing, the proper valve seat job can promote more efficient breathing by as much as 60%. The flow can be controlled, and altered, greatly by changing the valve seat widths and angles. Researchers have discovered and proven,

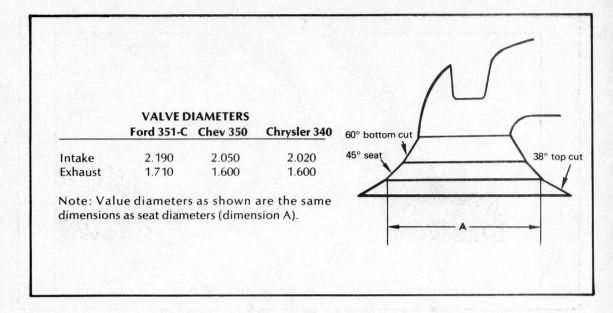

VALVE DIAMETERS			
	Ford 351-C	Chev 350	Chrysler 340
Intake	2.190	2.050	2.020
Exhaust	1.710	1.600	1.600

Note: Value diameters as shown are the same dimensions as seat diameters (dimension A).

for example, that a thicker seat passes more air than a thinner seat.

The bottom cut (of a three angle valve job) will direct the flow into the seat, and the top cut directs the flow past the seat and into the combustion chamber much like an air foil. The thought on exhaust valve seats is a 45° seat (.090″ wide) with a 38° top cut and a full blended radius replacing the bottom cut. This radius is generated as a series of angles in order to turn the exhaust flow. The intake valve seat is cut at a 45° angle, (.080″ wide) with a top cut at 38° and a bottom cut at 60°.

The rough valve seat is the first operation. The combustion chamber is roughly cleaned up, then the 45° seat is rough cut at a .010″ smaller diameter than the finished seat will be. A carbide cutting tool is employed which cuts all three angles at the same time on the rough valve job. The valve job must be in place first in order to be able to properly bring the ports into the seats and blend everything smoothly.

THE EXHAUST PORT

Production cylinder heads generally have less restrictive intake ports than exhaust ports, so the exhaust ports must receive much more work in order to achieve maximum breathing capacity.

A high velocity, good flowing exhaust port is essential with a competition engine when an improved (over stock) camshaft design increases the flow potential of the port. Good exhaust scavenging (or, the port acting as a vacuum to pull out gases) is important in order to achieve power gains.

The short side radius is one of the most important aspects of the exhaust port in terms of getting the gases out of the combustion chamber. This radius must be gentle—not sharp—so as not to create any unwanted turbulence. However, in many head designs, it acts as an impedence rather than a help. A gentle radius on the short side will help the flow by maintaining the rate of flow of the gases.

The shortest distance out of the exhaust port for the gases to flow is along the floor of the port, and naturally the gases will seek that shortest route. So the floor, as well as the short side radius, must receive development. Any time a port makes a severe directional change, port flow can benefit by the floor of the port being flat rather than rounded. The idea is that the flat floor reduces frictional resistance for the gases.

This development of the exhaust port floor and short side radius is limited by how much material is present in the head casting between the water jacket and the port. Usually, Detroit would rather sell you more water jacket space than cast iron, which makes you seek an alternative to just plain grinding. The answer, especially with the Ford 351-C and Chrysler 340 exhaust ports, is to add material to the exhaust floor by a welding process, then grind to reshape for a gentler contour. The low and mid-lift flow rates of the valve are es-

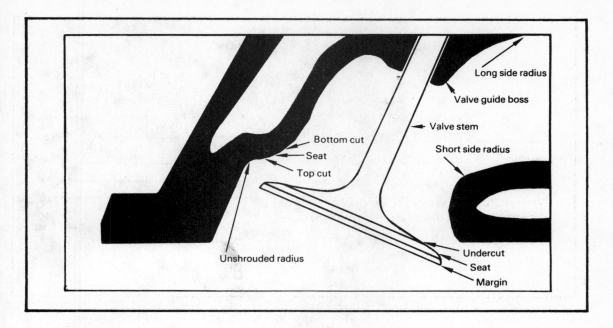

Long side radius

Valve guide boss

Valve stem

Short side radius

Bottom cut

Seat

Top cut

Undercut

Seat

Margin

Unshrouded radius

The seats are carefully finished with stones. CHA checks the accuracy of their stones before each head is cut.

The seat, bottom cut and top cut are all accurately measured with dividers.

With the finished port in the Chevy small block, the exhaust has almost a straight shot out of the combustion chamber.

The Chrysler 340 exhaust ports require extensive reshaping.

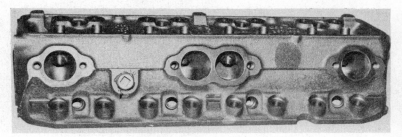

The old style of Chevrolet angle plug heads have round exhaust ports. The almost-square exhaust ports on the Chevy heads we illustrate are the new style, or turbo casting, heads.

pecially enhanced by raising the floor. Generally, at and near maximum valve lift, the port will be flowing more on the ceiling of the port.

THE INTAKE PORT

The big problem with contouring the ultimate intake port configuration is that the port is flowing two different materials—air and fuel. For most efficient combustion, the fuel must remain atomized in the air while it flows into the combustion chamber. The problem stems from the fact that the fuel wants to separate from the air everytime the mixture encounters a turn in direction or a change in velocity. The increased pressure on the mixture in these situations will want to leave the fuel behind and make the air surge ahead.

The way to keep the air and fuel from separating is to come up with a port configuration which has the flow velocity as equal as possible on the roof and floor of the port. How this is done can only be learned by making changes and checking the flow changes they make on a flow bench.

In the combustion chamber itself, as much turbulence as possible is desired to accelerate the rate of combustion. This is in contrast to flow in the ports where as little turbulence as possible is wanted. The combustion chamber turbulence starts from the back of the intake valve where the flow encounters the swirl polish on the valve. The top cut then directs the flow into the radius between the combustion chamber walls and roof. This radius, which should be wide and gentle, will swirl the mixture into the chamber.

THE VALVE GUIDE BOSS

The port flow can be helped by reducing the cross sectional area of the valve guide boss, as well as by smoothing it and by reducing its height. The valve guide boss must not, however, be completely ground away as it serves a very important purpose in stabilizing the valve stem. This helps reduce stem wear and it also reduces valve seat wear by guiding the valve head back down on its proper center.

For better port flow in the small block Chevy head, use a Moroso drive-in valve guide. The cast-in valve guide and boss can be completely removed, the guide drilled out to .500″ ID, then the guide is driven in.

WALL FINISH

Many people believe a properly ported head will have a mirror-bright finish on all the port walls, both intake and exhaust. This is not the

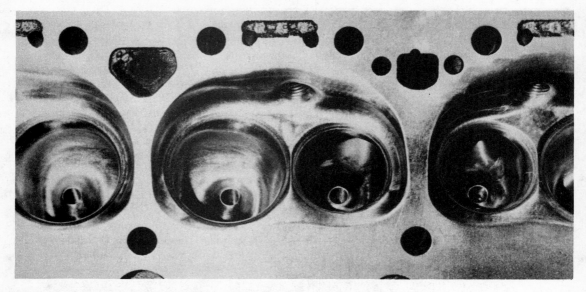

Notice how the valve guide boss has been reshaped to help air flow, yet retain as much support as possible for the valve stem. Also notice the almost flat port floor shape, and the metal finish.

case.

The intake ports should be finished with a 60 grit rotary stone, which leaves a fairly rough surface. The wet flow is better along this type of a surface so the air and fuel do not separate as much. A very polished finish in the intake port makes the fuel hang on the walls, creating a rich condition.

For dry flow in the exhaust ports, the walls should be very smooth to reduce frictional resistance on the gases, as well as making the wall surface difficult for carbon to accumulate on. Use a 240 grit rotary stone to finish the exhaust port walls.

In the combustion chamber, a glassy smooth finish is desired in order to promote turbulence. The combustion chamber should be finished with 240 grit stone.

BASIC HEAD PORTING

While much of the horsepower gain being experienced in today's sophisticated racing engines is the result of highly modified ports which can only be done by a cylinder head modification service, we can provide you with guidelines which will enable you to do a basic porting job yourself which will considerably improve the breathing of your cylinder heads. This outline of the basic methods should also improve your understanding of head porting.

The first step is to have the three-angle intake valve seat and two-angle exhaust valve seat roughed in. Nothing can be done until the exact location of these seats is known. Then all porting can be done up to the seats.

Each angle cut of the three-angle intake seat and two-angle exhaust seat leaves sharp edges. These edges should be blended into each other (just enough to remove the sharp edge), and blended into the port and combustion chamber with a rotary stone. The sharp edges which this operation gets rid of create abrupt changes in the flow path, which of course are undesirable.

The bottom cuts must be blended into the port walls. Use a rotary file for the initial metal removal, and finish it with a rotary stone.

The short side radius should be blended into the exhaust port valve pocket to provide a smooth turn for the gases. Remove the initial material with a rotary file, then finish with a rotary stone. Be careful here not to remove too much material and break through into the water jacket. CHA alters the short side radius by first adding more material with a welding process, then grinding and blending. If you should break through the port into the water jacket, purchase some Epon 907 from Diamond Racing which is an epoxy resin designed for just such occurrences. It can be ground and polished just like cast iron once it is dry. The only place it cannot be used is in extremely high temperature zones, such as the

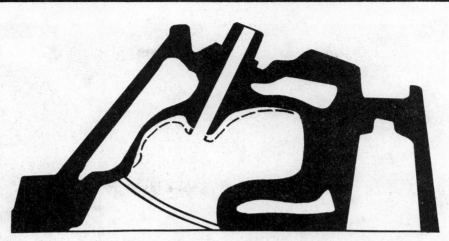

The Chevy 350 intake port. Above, dotted lines show original configuration of port. Solid black represents reworked port shape. Below, a cross-section of a stock port.

combustion chamber and exhaust port.

The long side radius of the exhaust port should be smoothed and blended into the valve pocket with a rotary stone. The amount of material removal all around the port is .080'' to .090'', depending on port wall thickness. This is standard on all intake and exhaust ports for small block engine heads.

In the combustion chamber area, start by laying a head gasket on the head surface and scribe the outline of the gasket around the combustion chamber opening. This scribe mark is vitally im-

portant because if you open up the chamber past the gasket surface, you have ruined the head. To prevent gasket sealing problems, keep the head surface intact at least .080'' inside the scribe mark all the way around. By the time you surface the head after porting, the gasket boundary will be about .100'' to .125'' outside the combustion chamber. Inside this scribe mark boundary, use a 60 grit rotary stone to unshroud the outside areas of both valves to promote better low lift valve flow. The metal finish in the combustion chamber should be mirror smooth, so finish it off with a

The Chevy 350 exhaust port. Above, a cross-section cut of a stock exhaust port can be seen, showing how much material is available for porting. Below left, the dotted lines show original configuration of stock port. Below right, the exterior of the exhaust port on the turbo casting. The dotted lines indicate original shape of port at mouth.

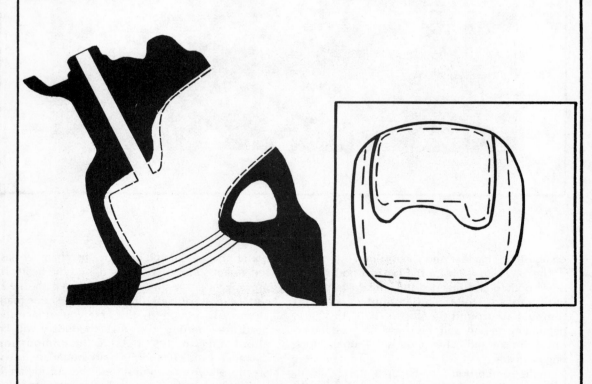

The Ford 351-C exhaust port. Above, the dotted lines show original configuration of port. The cross-section lines indicate the weld material added to short side radius. Below, a cross-section of a completed 351-C exhaust port. The black line shows what the original configuration of the port was.

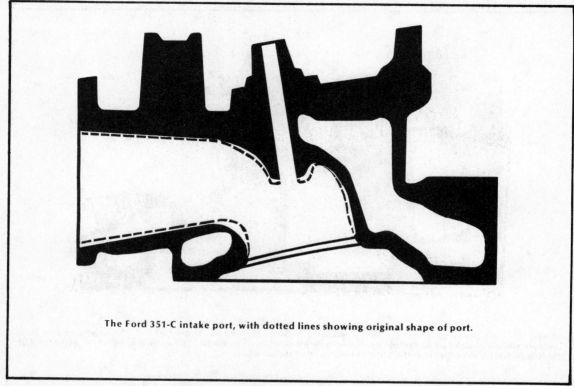

The Ford 351-C intake port, with dotted lines showing original shape of port.

fine grit rotary polishing stone (240 grit). A radi-used junction should be maintained between the roof and walls of the chamber. Be sure that every bump and contour in the combustion chamber is radiused and smoothed, not sharp. Sharp edges will create hot spots, which in turn can create preignition problems.

In the intake port, the seat grinding stones leave a sharp edge entering the port. Use a rotary stone to radius the sharp edges and blend them into the port. Remember these sharp edges create swirls and eddies in the incoming flow stream, which can severely impede the flow and cause air/fuel separation.

The long side radius of the intake port should be blended with a rotary stone up to the bottom cut. Just enough material to remove the sharp edges and rough casting should be ground away.

A blueprint guideline for the porting of the intake side of the Chevy 350 angle plug heads.

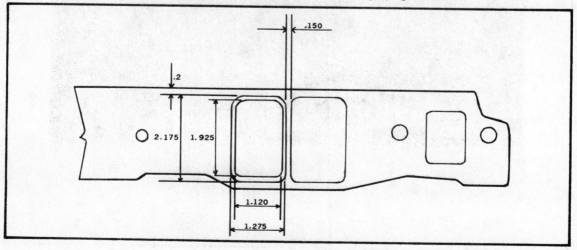

The Chrysler 340 intake port. Above, dotted lines indicate the original shape of the port. Below, a cross-section cut of a 340 head shows how much material is available for porting.

The Chrysler 340 exhaust port. This is another of the ports which can benefit greatly by adding weld material to the short side radius. Notice in the cross-section below how sharp the radius is exiting the valve pocket.

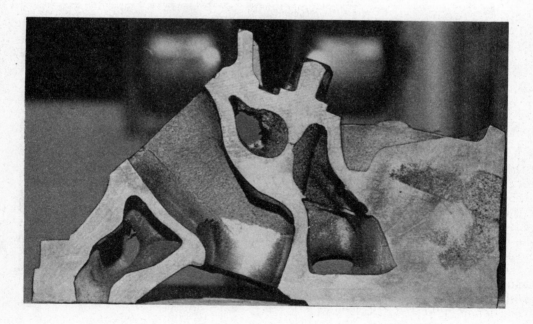

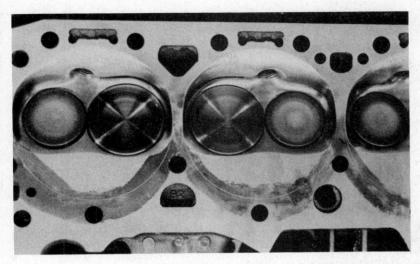

A finished Chevy 350 combustion chamber. Compare it with the stock chamber below.

The short side radius in the intake port should be blended in a smooth radius from the bottom cut to the port floor. Again, be careful not to remove too much material here.

The spark plug opening into the chamber should be radiused and blended into the chamber walls. The radius should extend at least into the first thread of the hole.

The roof of the combustion chamber should be radiused, smoothed and highly polished. The high polish promotes incoming air/fuel swirl.

The height of the valve guide bosses can be ground down a maximum of .375". The cross sectional diameter of the bosses can be reduced slightly in a radius that blends them smoothly into the port walls.

The cross sectional dimension of the port open-ings on the intake manifold side can be opened by about .180". Use a rough grit rotary stone for this. Blend this material removal into the port walls very smoothly with a rotary stone.

For more detailed information on how to con-tour the intake and exhaust ports of the Chevrolet, Chrysler and Ford heads, refer to the drawings and photos in this chapter.

To check the sealing capacity of your finished valve job, assemble the head just as it will be installed on the engine, then fill the ports (one at a time) with solvent. Any fluid leakage will indicate inadequate sealing. If you get a leak, lap the valve, then re-check with solvent. If the leak does not stop, use the seat cutting stones to retouch the seats.

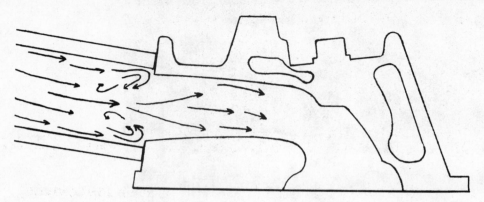

The drawing above shows with air flow arrows what can happen if the intake manifold ports are larger than the head ports. The flow meets a solid wall and is turned back, creating a very low flow. Below, the flow is as it should be with the head ports larger.

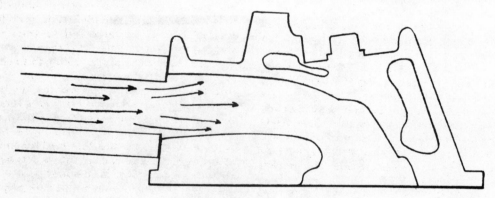

A cross section of an Edelbrock Torker manifold shows how the stock manifold mates to the head ports.

The MoPar 340 intake ports bene-fit by being opened up wide.

HEAD WELDING

Head welding is a very delicate process because the material being welded—cast iron—can warp and crack very easily during heating and cooling. The process requires a special torch and a powdered alloy material. The alloy filler material is contained in a cannister on the torch and is fed much like oxygen is fed into a cutting torch. Before any welding is done, the head is carefully heated to 500°F (this compares to 1400°F which some welding processes require). Then the torch is used to weld or build up extra material. Once the operation is completed, the head is completely wrapped in asbestos and placed in an oven where it is brought back to ambient temperature very gradually over a 24-hour period to prevent warping.

The welding process is used to weld shut heat riser passages as well as to build up material on the floor of the exhaust ports on some heads.

REVERSION CONTROL

During the overlap period of the camshaft, the entire induction and exhaust system is open to the atmosphere, from the carburetor air intake through the intake manifold, into the combustion chamber through the intake valve and out the chamber through the exhaust valve, and through the headers back to the atmosphere. During this condition, exhaust gases can be unpredictable and flow back into the induction areas, where they are not supposed to be. Reversion is this reverse flow pulsing. It contaminates the purity of the incoming air/fuel charge, and reduces the total amount of fresh air and fuel in the combustion chamber at the time of combustion. It is definitely detrimental to making horsepower.

Evidence of reversion is a soft, dark gray soot in the intake ports in the head, in the opening edges of the intake manifold, and in severe cases, in the

Notice how razor sharp the valve bottom cut edge becomes against the spark plug deflector. This is the reason the deflector must be welded over.

Weld material has been added in the Chevy 350 head spark plug deflectors.

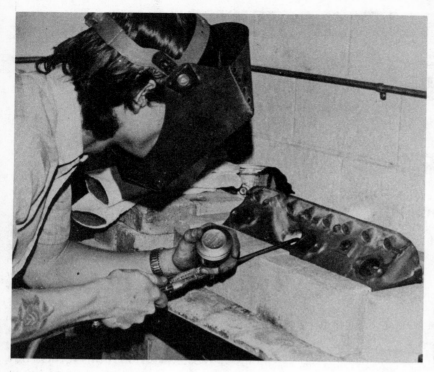

A technician welds the heat riser passage shut in an old style Chevy angle plug head (the new turbo castings do not have heat riser passages).

intake manifold runners.

To control reversion, some steps can be taken in the heads. The correct angle cuts of the top cuts and bottom cuts around the valves help keep the air flowing in the right direction. The correct angles, acting as air deflectors, will interrupt reversion. This is another reason why the valve seat angles are so vitally important.

Another way to interrupt reversion is to purposely mismatch the intake manifold runners with the head ports. The intake manifold runners must be slightly smaller all around than the head ports. This way, the incoming flow will just expand and flow very gracefully as it makes the transition from the smaller runners to the larger runners, but reverse flow gases, which are generally running along the roof or floor of the head ports, will run into an air dam (the intake manifold edges) and be bounced back into the combustion chamber again.

Reversion can also be controlled with the headers (see a discussion of this in the header chapter).

HEAD MILLING

In all cases, a milling cut must be made on the deck surface of the head to insure a straight, parallel surface, to decrease the combustion chamber CCs and to provide an adequately rough sealing surface for the head gasket. The maximum which should be milled off of any small block head is .060".

MAKING PORT MOLDS

If you are seriously interested in visually inspecting and studying cylinder head port shapes, contours and angles, there is a rubber foam avail-

The milling machine takes a cut off a cylinder head.

Combustion chamber molds, above, and port runner molds, below, which have been made by Pete Incaudo for study.

able from Dow Corning which you can easily use for this purpose. It is called Dow Corning S-5370 RTV foam. It comes in two parts, which are mixed together forming a liquid rubber substance. It is poured into the port or combustion chamber to be studied and sealed tight. The liquid expands and dries into a dense rubber. After a minute or so, the mold can be pulled out and inspected.

The port molds can help you spot abrupt changes in the port which could cause turbulence,

and it allows you to measure and duplicate a good working port. It also allows you to check if all ports are ground to the same configuration.

VALVE GUIDES

In stock form, the as-cast valve guides can give thousands of miles of good service, but in racing form, any head should have some work done to the valve guides. A brand new head can have the guides worn out in one or two races, so it is a good idea to rework the guides when the heads are brand new. An excellent reason for this is that a head can get weakened in the areas around the top of the valve guides because of the high spring pressures and high valve lift. The guide reworking tools could then crack the guides, so it is best to perform the work on a new head.

The best valve guide for all engines is the bronze wall guide, made by Winona. Most all engine machine shops are equipped to recondition valve guides with the Winona system, and the cost is relatively low. What the process consists of is tapping the stock guide with a course tap, and then threading the bronze wall guide (which is actually a fine-wound bronze wire) into the course threads. The interior of the bronze wall guide is then reamed to a size that will give a .0002" clearance between the guide and valve stem. This

Notice the rough surface left on the head by the milling machine. This gives the head gasket some tooth to bite into for a better seal. Notice also how the valve seat has been cut with just a single angle, and how the seat edges are very sharp.

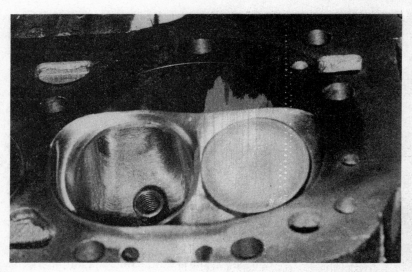

A Moroso valve guide has been installed in this Chevy head. Note how guide interior contains the same spiralling as a bronze wall bushing.

is a very tight clearance, but the tighter the clearance, the more concentric the valve seat will remain. As the bronze wall guide is grooved all the way down its length, it carries a sufficient supply of oil which the valve stem glides on.

For the Chevy 350 head, a new valve guide is on the market, being sold by Moroso. It serves all the purposes as the Winona guides we discussed above, but it is longer and thicker than a stock guide, thus giving much better support to the valve, insuring further against beating the seats out of the heads.

The guide is installed by first completely grinding away all of the stock cast-in guide in the head in both the ports and on top of the head. The guide hole is drilled out to .500″ ID. The new Moroso guide is then pressed in, and is held in place with an interference fit (the guide OD is .5025″). This guide has been tested in some Chevy 350 heads in Grand National super speedway racing, and has shown that it works exceptionally well.

The greatest beauty of the guide is that the stock cast-in valve guide bosses can be removed in the ports, allowing approximately a 15% gain in flow.

POSTING THE FORD BOSS HEADS

The Ford Boss 302 and 351-C cylinder heads have a unique problem. That is, they are of a very thin casting, and the water jacket area comprises a large portion of the head. When these heads are used in competition where combustion temperatures are high and the cylinder compression is high, the head begins to flex and force out water.

The water may be forced out at the radiator, or from around the head gasket.

To cure this problem, the heads must be posted. The posts installed in the heads function virtually the same as timbers used to shore up tunnels. What the posts do is support the combustion area of the head against deflection.

The materials required to post one head are: four 5/16″-18 bolts 1″ long, four 3/8″-16 cup point set screws 2½″ long, one number F drill, one 5/16″ drill, one 3/8″ diameter end mill, and Loctite.

The support of the posts is added at three separate areas of the head, thus three separate machining set-ups are required: 1) Top side of the head through three intake rocker stud holes, 2) One end of the head, and 3) In four places through the combustion chamber side of the head.

The first operation requires locating the intake rocker stud boss correctly. First, locate the head so it is true with the length (in a parallel measurement) of the machining table. The intake ports of the head should be facing toward the machine operator. Bolt the head down securely through two head bolt holes, one at each end of the head.

The intake rocker stud is machined on a compound angle. These two angles should be located accurately. The purpose for this is to drill a 5/16″ hole through the existing threaded rocker stud hole into the water jacket and anchored into the metal on the other side (no deeper). It is now tapped for the 3/8″-16 x 2½″ set screws. Since the rocker stud is 7/16″-14, the set screw just barely has the clearance required to be screwed into the tapped hole. A long Allen wrench is needed to

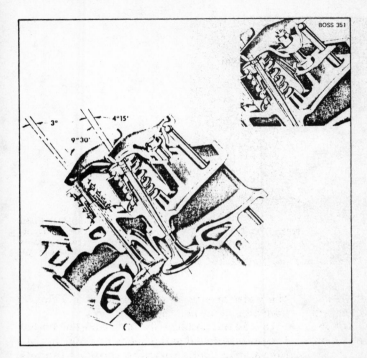

BOSS 351

Left, the compound angles of the Ford 351-C valves. Below, an illustration of how a set screw is installed through a rocker stud hole to brace the water jacket of the head.

tighten the set screw firmly in the head, thus providing the additional support to the combustion chamber area. In simple terms, all you have is a threaded hole (the 3/8''-16 set screw) inside another threaded hole (the 7/16''-14 rocker stud hole). Only three of the four intake stud holes are used. The second intake stud hole from the left (with the intake ports facing out towards the machine operator) is not drilled because the set

screw would only enter the heat riser passage, not providing any meaningful support.

After drilling and tapping these three holes on one head, remove the head and bolt the other head in place. Since we are dealing with compound angles, the set-up time is reduced to a minimum by using the same machine set-up for this operation.

The last of the four set screws is installed in the

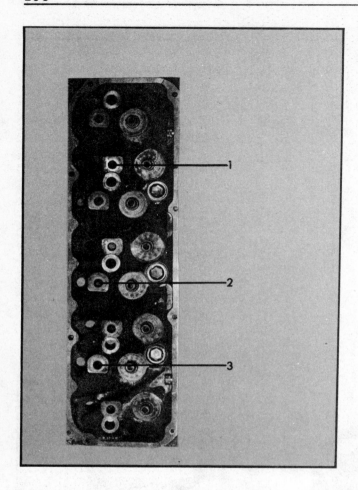

This is where the three top-mounted 3/8''-16 set screws are drilled and threaded on the 351-C.

The first set-up of the machining operation. The compound intake stud angle is picked up, then the Bridgeport mill drills through stud hole into water jacket.

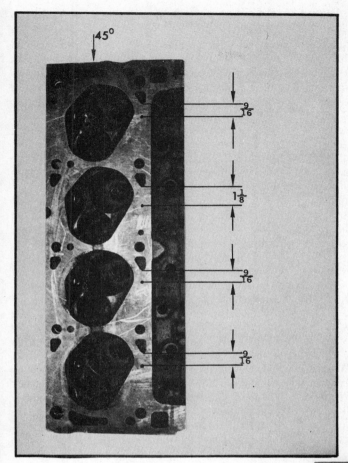

From the combustion chamber side, this is where the four bolt holes are drilled. Note that spacing is taken from water passage holes. The 45° angle location is also indicated.

The location of the 45° angle bolt.

The Bridgeport mill first spots the bolt hole location with a 3/8″ end mill, then drills hole with a 5/16″ drill.

second machining operation. A 3/8"-16 hole is tapped at a 45° angle to the end of the head. With the exhaust ports facing out toward the machine operator, this operation is performed at the right end of the head. Before bolting the head down into position, the end of the head (in the general area of the intake valve) must be marked with machinist's blue dye. A line is scribed to locate the hole to be drilled. Bolt the head down securely and locate the scribed line. With the 3/8" end mill, spot face the head for the 5/16" drill. Remember the hole is to be drilled at a 45° angle to the head, so spot facing the head is the only way the hole can be drilled. Again, drill through the head with the 5/16" drill until it breaks through the water jacket into the metal on the other side of it. Tap and insert the last set screw. Tighten it firmly, but do not over-tighten.

In the third machining operation, the combustion chamber area of the head is given added support by drilling and tapping four 5/16"-18 holes. These holes are to be drilled outside of the actual combustion chamber area of the head. The reason is that heat from combustion could cause a water leak and a compression loss.

The small cast water passages in the head are used as the locating points for the holes to be drilled. Drill and tap into the water jacket for the 5/16"-18 bolts following the dimensional diagram. Notice the distance varies for hole number two. Remember in operation number one, we omitted drilling the second intake valve stud hole because of drilling into the heat riser passage. By using the 1-1/8" distance from the edge of the cast hole, the entire section can be supported. After firmly tightening all four bolts, cut them off even with the head. The head should then be resurfaced on a head milling machine.

All of the machine operations outlined above are performed on a Bridgeport mill. All threaded bolts and holes should be thoroughly cleaned with lacquer thinner and coated with Loctite before bolting. All of the bolts and screws should have their threads flattened slightly in one or two places by tapping lightly with a hammer. This creates a type of interference thread that will not back out or work loose. It also serves to hold the bolts securely until the Loctite dries.

CC'ING THE HEADS

The term "CC" stands for cubic centimeter, and by CCing the heads, you are determining the volume of each combustion chamber in cubic centimeters.

In a high performance engine where all the horsepower you can get is vital, it is important that all of the combustion chambers be equal in volume. If they are not, the individual cylinders will vary in compression ratio, and the cylinders will not all be doing the same amount of work. Checking for an even amount of chamber volume, then, is the major reason for CCing the heads, with the operation also being important to determining the compression ratio of the engine. Although both operations are painstaking, both must be done on a high performance engine if the best in performance can be expected from it.

Begin your CCing operation with the heads assembled as they are going to be installed on the block. The CCing operation is the final one performed on the heads before they are installed. Begin with the heads lying on a flat surface, combustion chamber up. Either the intake ports or exhaust ports should be on an angle slightly uphill. This helps facilitate the chamber filling.

The tools required are a chemist's burette and a clear plastic plate (such as Plexiglass). The burette is a long clear tube with CC's graduated in small increments on its side, and a filling valve on its end. The plastic plate should be at least ½" thick so it does not deflect easily, and should be at least two inches larger than the combustion chamber area in all directions. This makes sure the plate adequately covers and seals on the chamber.

The head surface should be coated with a light film of grease to seal the plate, then the plastic plate is pressed over the chamber. The plate must have a hole in it just large enough for the burette to discharge fluid into the chamber. The fluid to be used in the burette is clean solvent, colored with a red food coloring to make reading the gradations on the burette easier.

Plexiglass plate is installed over bore and sealed tight with grease in order to measure cc's. Plate has to be deep enough to clear dome of piston.

When the burette is full, it will read zero CCs. As the solvent is discharged into the chamber through the plate, the level will fall. When the chamber is completely full, simply read the graded markings on the burette to learn how many CCs of fluid the chamber holds. When filling the chamber, be sure the solvent does not leak out of the seal between the head and the plastic plate. If it does, reseal the plate and start over. Also, be sure all of the air bubbles get out of the fluid in the chamber. Air bubbles displace volume, so they will give you a false reading.

All of the combustion chambers should hold the same volume in the best of conditions. In all likelihood, this will not happen. But, the chambers should all be within 1 CC of each other. If they are not, the lower volume chambers must be reworked to conform to the highest volume chamber. Metal must be removed in the chamber to equalize the CCs. Do not sink the valves further into the head to equalize the chambers. Instead, make precise measurements between the highest and lowest

volume chambers, and determine what the difference in chamber configuration is that causes a difference in volume.

In stock form, the combustion chamber CCs are as follows for the cylinder head part numbers we have specified:

Chevy 350	Chrysler 340	Ford 351-C
67-69 CCs	69-74 CCs	64-67 CCs

In racing forms, the combustion chambers for these heads should CC out to:

Chevy 350	Chrysler 340	Ford 351-C
66 CCs	66 CCs	63 CCs

DETERMINING THE COMPRESSION RATIO

Although the pistons you purchased to go along with your bore and particular cylinder heads are supposed to give you a certain compression ratio, you cannot be sure without first checking it. And of course, you must be sure of the compression ratio in order to determine the best timing ad-

Wilson uses a chemist's burette to measure volume of chamber created by the piston flat being below the deck surface at TDC. This is considered part of cylinder chamber volume when computing compression ratio.

vance in order to avoid detonation.

The first thing which must be computed is the cubic inches per cylinder. This is done with the following formula:

$$(bore)^2 \times .7854 \times stroke = cubic\ inches$$

From this formula, also, you can determine the total cubic inches of your engine by multiplying the answer by the number of cylinders in the engine.

The next thing which must be known is the piston dome deck height volume. This will tell you how much volume the piston pushes above the block. To check this volume, a two piece plastic plate must be constructed and glued together. The first piece of plastic is sufficiently thick to reach above the piston dome when the plastic is placed on the cylinder deck and the piston is at TDC. The plastic is bored out in the center the same as the cylinder bore. Then a solid piece of plastic is glued on top of it to make a sealed container which fits over the cylinder. Drill a small hole in the top of the plastic plate in order to be able to fill it with fluid.

To measure the piston dome displacement volume, first take the piston down to BDC and apply a light film of grease evenly around the cylinder. This assures a tight seal. Then bring the piston up to TDC, using a dial indicator to be sure true TDC is found. Wipe off all the excess grease squeezed up by the piston. Grease the mating surface of the plastic plate which will be sealing the cylinder bore and place the plastic on the deck over the piston. Be sure you have a tight seal. Use the chemist's burette to fill the plastic plate. Again, be sure there are no air bubbles in the fluid. Then subtract the number of CCs of fluid that filled the plastic from the total volume (in CCs) of the plastic plate when it is empty. The answer you get is the number of CCs the piston dome pushes above the deck. On the sample Chevy 350 engine we built for this book, the total CCs of the plastic plate used was 139.1. The volume of fluid we put into the plastic when it was placed on the cylinder was 126.6 CCs. The volume which this piston pushed above the block, then, is 12.5 CCs.

The next step is to determine the number of CCs which the head gasket will hold. It can be measured physically by being placed between two plastic plates and being filled with fluid. The easiest way, though, is to calculate it mathematically. The formula for this would be the volume of a cylinder (in CC's), or:

$$16.387 \times 3.14 \times (radius)^2 \times (thickness) = volume$$

For the gasket we specified for the Chevy 350, the volume of the gasket compressed is 4.1 CCs, and

being two are used in a sandwich, the gasket volume is 8.2 CCs.

The cylinder head CCs are added to the gasket CCs, then the volume which the piston pushes above the deck is subtracted from this answer. In our example engine, the combustion chamber is 66.6 CCs, and the gasket volume is 8.2 CCs, so the total is 74.8 CCs. The piston is pushing 12.5 CCs above the deck, so this subtracted from 74.8 equals 62.3 CCs. This amount (the 62.3 CCs) is called the dead volume.

Next, the live volume must be found. The number of cubic inches per cylinder is converted to CCs by dividing the cubic inches by .061. For our example engine, the cubic inches per cylinder are 44.75, and divided by .061, this gives us 734 CCs. This is the live volume which is compressed into the combustion chamber.

Add the dead volume and live volume together, and you get a total cylinder CC volume. Divide the total cylinder CCs by the dead volume, and the answer is the compression ratio.

For our example engine, 734 CCs (one cylinder) plus 62.3 CCs (dead volume) equals 796.3 CCs. 796.3 divided by 62.3 equals 12.7, which is the compression ratio. This compression ratio worked out to be a couple of percentage points higher than was expected, and higher than was really desired.

Headers

A steel tubular open exhaust system is mandatory to extract maximum torque and horsepower from any competition engine. Primary and secondary tube lengths and diameters can vastly alter the engine performance derived from the tuned exhaust system. A competition engine can never reach its full potential without an exhaust system which is fine-tuned to the application (RPM range and torque range).

Tuned headers help scavenge burnt exhaust gases from the combustion chamber, creating a vacuum behind them from the fast exit. This allows the incoming fresh charge of air/fuel a great boost in filling the combustion chambers more effectively. Improperly chosen headers can, just like stock cast iron exhaust manifolds, cause a back pressure which can prevent all of the burnt exhaust gas from escaping. In this case, the burnt gases left behind will dilute the incoming fuel/air charge, naturally causing a reduction in power output with that charge.

Which diameter/length combination provides the greatest exhaust gas exit speed depends on the cubic inch displacement and the RPM operating range of the engine. Different length/diameter combinations will produce different RPM ranges of maximum torque output. Collector (or secondary pipe) lengths also have a bearing on the primary diameter/length combination.

WHICH SIZE IS BEST?

Through dynomometer testing of various combinations for the 350-cubic inch displacement engines (this includes, the MoPar 340 and Ford 351, or any engine between 340 and 360 cubic inches), Wilson has found the following to be the most profitable combinations: For short tracks, up to 5/8th-mile, the best diameter is 1 ¾ '' with a primary length of 30 to 32 inches. For longer tracks, such as superspeedways or any place where a narrow torque band in a high RPM range is desired, a 2'' diameter primary pipe with a length of 38 inches is recommended.

Dyno tests have shown that narrower, longer primary tubes move the torque peak into a lower RPM range. The shorter, wider pipes peak the torque at a higher range.

In building the headers, all tube lengths should be equal in length, with no critical bends. A variance among lengths of 2 inches is very significant, and should be avoided.

If you have an engine of a different cubic inch

displacement, or want to determine a different diameter or length, there are two formulas which can help you closely approximate the correct answer. They are:

$$\text{Primary pipe diameter} = \sqrt{\frac{CI \times 1900}{L \times RPM}}$$

(L = primary pipe length)

$$\text{Primary pipe length} = \frac{CI \times 1900}{D^2 \times RPM}$$

(D = primary pipe diameter)

THE COLLECTOR OR SECONDARY PIPE

From the point where all four primary pipes are collected into a single exhaust outlet until the pipe ends is considered the entire collector length. For engines in the 340 to 360 cubic inch group, the collector tailpipe should be 3¼ inches in diameter, up to 36 inches of total length. If the collector tailpipe is longer than 36 inches, then the entire length of the pipe should be 3½ inches in diameter.

A crossover pipe, which equalizes exhaust pressure, should be installed between the two collector tailpipes anywhere from 3 to 12 inches behind the start of the collector. The crossover pipe should be a minimum of 2½ inches in diameter, and 3 inches at best.

WHERE TO GET 'EM

The two best sources of custom headers for oval track and road racing are Stahl and Kustom (addresses are listed in the appendix in the back of the book). Both of these companies have extensive experience in this field and this application, and can provide headers for most common engines, oil pans, frames and clearances. These people also have done extensive dyno and field research to be sure the product works. Nobody has to worry about the workmanship on these brands, either.

Another company which is beginning to enter the oval track racing field is Hooker. They are bending good headers with the particular clearance, etc., problems in mind which oval track stockers face. Their product is excellent, too.

If you are faced with a budget problem for a set of good headers, investigate Appliance. For the price they make a good set of headers with individual flanges on each pipe. Their primary market, though, is for aftermarket application on cars for the street, so consult with them for the model which will fit your car.

A word is in order about the maintenance of headers. First, they should be torqued down tight to the flange plate or head **after** they have cooled.

These header opening ports demonstrate what you get when you buy at a bargain price. Notice how ports are irregularly formed in the flange. So as not to impede exhaust flow, these must be ground smooth and straight to match head ports.

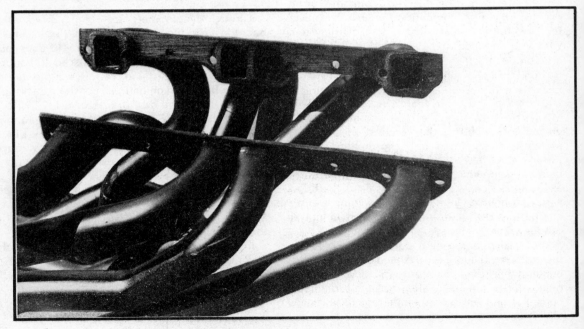

Typical installation of a header flange plate. Notice how flange openings and bolt patterns allow larger header tube diameter.

This should be done several times after new headers have been installed, until the headers take a set. Continued checking for tightness is important to prevent header and flange warping. When the headers are disconnected, such as when engine or head changes are made, use a large flat file to keep the mating surfaces flat. A warpage problem can cause the header gasket to blow out.

There is a lot to be said about painting headers. Jack Davis of Hooker Headers has told us that to stay away from any of the controversies of painting, he gives the headers a final acid bath and lets the customer decide what he wants to do. A lot of racers say that the only paint to use is the Sperex white. This is a fine paint. It keeps the pipes from rusting, and at the same time, puts a protective heat barrier on them which keeps the exhaust heat inside the pipe instead of radiating into the engine compartment. No matter what color and type of paint you feel is best, at least paint your headers. They will wear a lot better.

REVERSION CONTROL

As more fully explained in the cylinder heads chapter elsewhere in this book, reversion is the reverse exhaust gas flow into the intake.

Much of the prevention of reversion can be accomplished with header flanges, or reversion plates. These are flat steel plates which are bolted to the exhaust ports on the heads, and then the headers are bolted to the plates. The reversion plates allow larger diameter header pipes to be installed, and they act as air dams against exhaust gas which is trying to flow back into the head during the overlap period of the camshaft. The port openings of the reversion plates are larger than the port openings in the head, but smaller than the header pipes, thus the gas flowing in reverse will meet a solid wall of resistance.

Engine Assembly

We have thoroughly discussed the preparation of all components you will be putting into your engine, so now it is time to get it altogether.

Engine assembly is not an overnight or weekend job, but rather a very time consuming and meticulous job. It takes Wilson about 25 hours to completely assemble an engine **after** all of the preparatory work has been done, and he is a man who has built thousands of racing engines. If you do not have this backlog of experience, it should take you even longer.

All of the parts you are going to be assembling, starting with the bare block on the engine stand, should be close at hand, clean and ready to go. A good tip is that all parts, such as rods, pistons, crank, etc., should be kept covered with airtight plastic once they are ready to go. This keeps them sanitary while other work is being performed.

INSTALLING THE CRANK

The first component to be laid into the bare block will be the crankshaft. Before installing the upper halves of the main bearing inserts, clean them off (front and back) with a clean cloth and lacquer thinner. Then generously oil the bearings before the crank goes in. All parts, as they are laid

in the block, should be generously oiled with the same oil which will be used in the crankcase (Wilson uses Union 20W-50 racing oil). Lay the crank in place and turn it with your hand to be sure it rotates freely with no bind. If the clearances have already been figured right and the crank

When bearing inserts are installed, they should be cleaned with lacquer thinner.

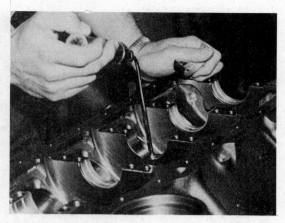

Wilson uses an inspection light to make one last check before crank is installed to be sure there is no debris in oil galleys which could damage or destroy bearings.

The main bearings are thoroughly lubed before the crank is bolted in place.

The thrust bearing is torqued in place while the screwdriver holds the crank end play in place.

journals and block have been prepared carefully, there will be no problem. After rotating, the crank is picked up and the main bearings are checked for any small particles which have scratched the bearings.

The rear main oil seal (always a neoprene type, never a rope type) is installed at an angle (see photo) so it lines up in the cap easily when the cap is installed. Then the lower bearing halves are inserted in the main caps, oiled, and placed on the crank. The bolts are torqued down in small increments. In the case of the Chevy 350 we assembled as a sample engine for this book, the long bolts on the caps received 70 ft/lbs of torque, and the short ones received 65 ft/lbs. (See the critical torque chart for complete torque informa-

tion on all engines).

Before the thrust bearing cap is torqued in place, the crankshaft end play must be checked. A large screwdriver acts as a wedge to push the crank forward in the block while a dial indicator at the rear of the block measures the crank's travel. When the proper end play is achieved, the thrust bearing cap is torqued with the screwdriver still in place. Then main bearing cap bolt torque is checked once again. "You can never go wrong by re-checking every operation you've done," says Wilson.

Next, the rods are attached to the pistons. The pins and rod bushings are liberally coated with oil before assembly. The Spirolox pin retainers are slipped in place, and the pin is checked for end

Notice how rear main oil seal has been installed with parting edge above bearing web surface.

play. Zero pin end play is desired, but not so snug that the pin cannot rotate.

INSTALLING THE PISTONS

The safest and easiest way to install a piston is with a tapered sleeve on top of the bore. The one Wilson uses he machined from mild steel. It is 6" tall and starts with a 4.25" ID at the top and tapers down to a 4.005" ID at the bottom (for the Chevy 350). This method makes it easy to install the pistons without nicking the rings on the block.

Some type of protective instrument has to be used over the exposed rod bolts as the piston/rod assembly is lowered into the bore, so the bolts do not scratch the crankshaft journals. A piece of rubber fuel line works well. What Wilson uses is a long brass shaft which is drilled and threaded on one end so it screws onto a rod bolt. This way the assembly can be inserted into the bore and he can reach around the block and grab the brass shaft as it protrudes, long before the piston starts its entry into the bore.

Rotate each ring on each piston a full revolution just before inserting it in the bore. This can show up a nick or burr in the ring groove. The rings should rotate freely.

Once the pistons are in and the rod caps bolted in place, rotate the crank and check for clearances (rod bolt to block and rod cap to block). These clearances should be at least .060".

The next step is to measure the rod small end clearance, from the side of the rod to the piston pin boss. This clearance has to be at least .100" or the rod will knock the pins out.

After the piston and rod installation, the deck clearance is checked once again. Then the crank is rotated several times by hand. The rod caps are taken off and the rod bearings are inspected for any nicks or scratches. If all bearings are fine, reinstall the caps and torque the rod bolts.

The rings are well oiled before the piston is installed.

The easy way to install piston/ring assembly is with a tapered installer. You should be able to push the assembly through with your hand without the aid of a hammer. If a hammer is required, something is wrong [check your rings].

The rod bolt clearance [against the block] should be checked when the trial fit is made of components [as described in the block chapter of this book]. If using other than stock rods, the Chevy small block must be ground for clearance at the crankcase for sufficient operating room for the rod bolt.

If a scratch is found on a bearing, look for a little piece of sand, metal, etc., on the journal. If none is visually present, run your fingers around the bearing to find a small particle imbedded in it. If no particle is found, then suspect a nick in the journal. To check for this, get a new bearing and run it around the journal by hand with a medium pressure, then inspect for scratches.

Torquing the rod bolts is a very intricate and time consuming operation. There are always two torquing specifications for a rod bolt: torque in ft/lbs and bolt stretch in inches. The rod manufacturer will always specify the torque with the rod. Before you begin torquing a rod bolt, check its length with a micrometer and write it down.

The brass guide tube protrudes from the bore as a piston and rod assembly is inserted. Note how rods and their caps have cylinder numbers engraved on each. No chance of anything getting mixed up this way.

One big mistake that most engine builders make is to get the rod small end too close to the piston pin boss. The minimum clearance, as being checked here with a feeler gauge, is .100 to .150". If the clearance is too small, machine the necessary material off the side of the small end of the rod. This clearance is mandatory to prevent the pin locks from being knocked out.

The side clearance between the pair of rods is held in place with metal feeler gauge strips while the rod bolts are torqued.

Torque to the rod manufacturer's specifications in small increments on each bolt on one rod, then mike the bolt length again to check for bolt stretch. For the sample engine we built for this book, Carillo rods were used, and the specifications were: 52 ft/lbs of torque and a stretch of from .006" to .007".

If the rod bolt does not stretch enough, unbolt it and put some Molykote under the bolt threads. If the rod bolt stretches too much, throw it away. Suspect that the threads are bad or the bolt material is weak. If the rod bolt will not stretch, that is an indication it is too hard and brittle (probably from improper heat treat), and should be properly placed in a trash can. All rod bolts and nuts should be thoroughly oiled before installing.

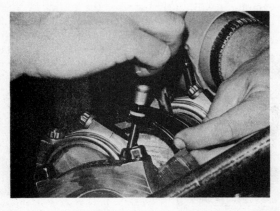

Wilson uses a ratchet micrometer to measure rod bolt stretch while torquing bolts.

CAMSHAFT INSTALLATION
Prepare the camshaft for its break-in run by painting all the lobes with Dow Corning Molykote. It is a molybdenum disulphide type of grease. Do not use this grease on the camshaft bearing journals. The Molykote will plug the oil feed holes to

The rear cam plug should be driven in backwards, then sealed with silicone rubber. This allows more clearance between cam and plug. When the cam is slid in place, it should be pushed all the way back against plug. When this is done, the front of the cam should be recessed 1/8" into block.

The camshaft lobes are thoroughly painted with a coat of Dow Corning Molykote. Cam bearing journals are not coated, as the Molykote could block oil feed holes to the cam bearings.

the cam bearings and cause an immediate bearing galling problem on the cam. For this same reason, do not paint the lobes with an excessive amount of Molykote. Just before the cam is inserted into the block, coat it liberally with GM's E.O.S. (Engine Oil Supplement, which is available at Chevy parts departments). The E.O.S. is, by the way, the only oil additive which Wilson feels should ever be used in a competition engine.

Push the cam into the block, being very careful not to nick any cam bearings or journals. For the last third of the way into the block, support the cam with a screwdriver. If you push the cam all the way by hand, you will not have it supported as it approaches the last journal, and it can slip down and nick a journal or a lobe. After the cam is all the way in, be sure it rotates freely by hand.

On a Chevy 350, use a cam thrust wear plate (made by Cloyes). Check to be sure its thickness is about .030". Whatever the plate's thickness is, this amount **must** be machined off the back of the cam gear so the timing gears will line up. Cloyes does not machine the gear for you. On the Ford, 351-C (or any Ford engine), machine .005" off the back of the cam thrust plate which bolts to the block. This is done to give the cam enough end play which a racing condition requires.

Install the timing gears and chain. On all three engines, Wilson recommends and uses Cloyes gears and roller chains. After they are tightened down, be sure they are lubricated well. The front of the engine is one of the last places to receive oil when the engine is turned over. Oil must penetrate into the spaces between the link plates on the timing chain to lubricate its bearing surfaces. A dry timing chain means it will tighten up and then lengthen.

The next step is the degreeing of the cam. This procedure has been thoroughly discussed in the camshaft chapter elsewhere in this book.

When using a cam timing bushing on the cam gear, securely bolt down the gear on the cam first, then slip on the bushing. This is a safety precaution which insures the timing is not going to be accidentally changed.

After cam degreeing is completed, move the degree wheel to the number one cylinder TDC mark before the wheel is taken off so the timing marks on the crank damper can be lined up accurately with the pointer.

Glue the timing cover gasket on the cover itself before installing it. Prior to attaching the cover, be sure to oil the crankshaft seal.

The damper (or harmonic balancer) is installed, being sure the inner and outer shaft is liberally

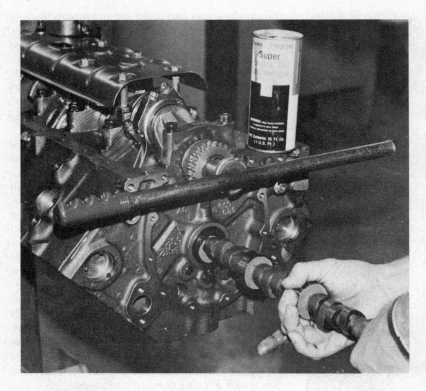

Wilson douses the cam with EOS before installing it.

For the last part of its insertion into the block, the cam is supported by a screwdriver so it won't drop and nick a journal or cam bearing.

When the timing gears are driven on, a screwdriver is inserted between a counterweight and a main bearing cap so the force of the hammer is not taken by the thrust bearing. This is an important step in saving the life of the thrust bearing.

The vibration damper is pulled in place with a nut, not driven on. Notice damper has been grooved to indicate timing marks.

The water pump is the next component to be installed. Ford and Chevrolet water pumps each have one bolt which protrudes into the water jacket. To prevent leaks, seal the bolt with silicone rubber (use Dow Corning 732 RTV adhesive sealant) before installing the bolt. As a safety precaution for proper cam end play, glue a piece of rubber on the cam cover which the water pump will keep in place.

With the cam in, the fuel pump push rod can be installed, well lubed of course. Many people do not think of it, but this lever should be Magnafluxed. Before installing the fuel pump, rotate the engine so the cam lobe is at its lowest point, making the fuel pump easier to install.

The oil pan is the next component to be installed. Wilson uses the Fel Pro gaskets here, with some silicone rubber sealant used **sparingly** between the gasket and the pan. Put the pan and its gasket on, and torque the bolts down half way, just enough to put an indentation in the gasket. Then remove the pan and put the silicone rubber sealant around the outside of that indented ridge. If too much sealant is used, it can squeeze out into the engine where it can get knocked off and find its way down to the oil pickup--and you know what will happen next. Just before the pan is attached, look everything over real well, then give the oil pump a few priming squirts of oil.

lubed. When the damper is driven on, use a screwdriver to take up the crank end play so you are not hammering on the thrust bearing. Once the damper is started, use a bolt to pull it onto the crank.

Check the end play of the camshaft with a screwdriver. It should be .006". Be carefull not to gouge the cam.

INSTALLING THE LIFTERS

The most important step before the lifters are installed is to check them for a radius on their cam contacting end. Lay a staight edge across the face to check the radius. This radius is designed into

The bottom end of this Ford 351-C engine reveals a nodular iron crank, Crower rods and Venolia pistons.

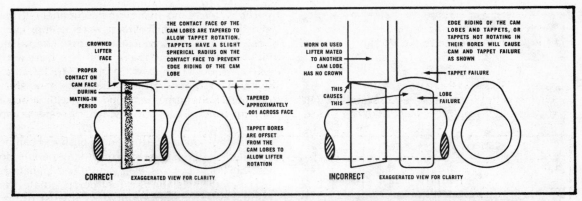

CROWNED
LIFTER
FACE

PROPER
CONTACT ON
CAM FACE
DURING
MATING-IN
PERIOD

THE CONTACT FACE OF THE
CAM LOBES ARE TAPERED TO
ALLOW TAPPET ROTATION.
TAPPETS HAVE A SLIGHT
SPHERICAL RADIUS ON THE
CONTACT FACE TO PREVENT
EDGE RIDING OF THE CAM
LOBE

TAPERED
APPROXIMATELY
.001 ACROSS FACE

TAPPET BORES
ARE OFFSET
FROM THE
CAM LOBES TO
ALLOW LIFTER
ROTATION

CORRECT   EXAGGERATED VIEW FOR CLARITY

WORN OR USED
LIFTER MATED
TO ANOTHER
CAM LOBE
HAS NO CROWN

THIS
CAUSES
THIS

EDGE RIDING OF THE CAM
LOBES AND TAPPETS, OR
TAPPETS NOT ROTATING IN
THEIR BORES WILL CAUSE
CAM AND TAPPET FAILURE
AS SHOWN

TAPPET FAILURE

LOBE
FAILURE

INCORRECT   EXAGGERATED VIEW FOR CLARITY

This drawing [courtest of Iskenderian Cams] illustrates why a radius on a tappet is so vital to its longevity.

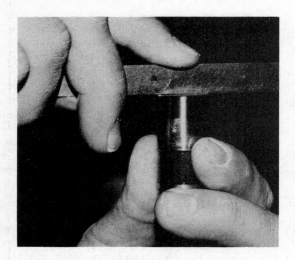

Above, the radius of the lifter bottom is checked with a steel straight edge. If the radius isn't there, toss the lifter away as a flat bottom tappet will wear cam lobe.

the lifter face so it does not wear the cam lobe.

To prepare the surface of the lifters, put them in a lathe at high speed and just **touch** the cam contact surface of the lifter with #600 grit wet sand paper to polish it. Before the lifters are slipped into the bore, paint the cam contact ends with Molykote.

When slipping the lifters in, be sure the fit is not snug. They should move in the lifter bores very easily.

The lifters are well coated over their entire surface with GM's E.O.S. when being installed, then the remaining E.O.S. in the can is poured into the lifter galley.

A Stahl valley oil baffle is installed to keep hot oil off the bottom of the intake manifold (these baffles are also available from Milodon and Mr.

The oil valley baffle is installed. It guards against hot oil splashing against the intake manifold, keeping the incoming air/fuel charge cooler.

Gasket). The retainers of the baffle are tucked under the heads rather than being compressed by the intake manifold to make intake manifold changes easier.

INSTALLING THE HEADS

On our sample engine, Milodon screw-in 7/16" studs were Loctited and screwed into the block.

However, if you use this method and develop a head gasket sealing problem, it could be that when the studs are torqued onto the block, the block deck surface is "ant-hilling". That is, the metal around the studs is being pulled upward slightly in a mound shape. If this is the case, the stock head bolts can be used successfully. Wilson is using them presently on all engines he is

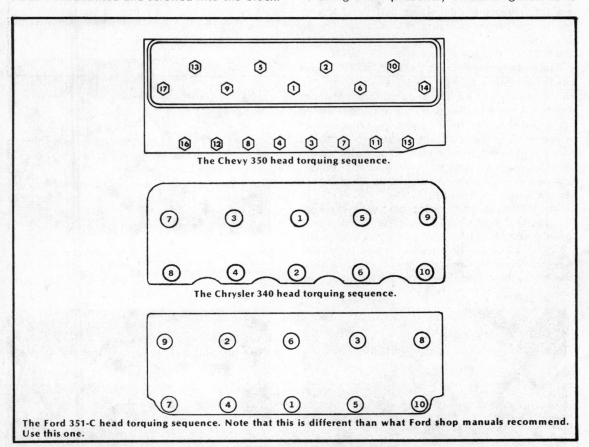

The Chevy 350 head torquing sequence.

The Chrysler 340 head torquing sequence.

The Ford 351-C head torquing sequence. Note that this is different than what Ford shop manuals recommend. Use this one.

Head studs, shown here, are preferred to factory-type head bolts. While they make heads hard to remove, they are best for positive gasket sealing. They are sold by Milodon and Mr. Gasket.

building. A further advantage of the stock type head bolts is that it is easier to disassemble and remove a head. With either type of stud on the Chevy, the long studs get 70 ft/lbs of torque and the short ones get 60 ft/lbs.

On the Chevrolet 350, Wilson uses **two** head gaskets **per side** (Chevrolet part number 3916336) with a light coating of aluminum paint as a sealant. The heads are then torqued down according to the proper torquing sequence (see drawings). The torque is applied in three separate applications of approximately 20 ft/lbs each.

The carburetor heating passages from the heads must be sealed to keep heat away from the manifold gasket and to keep the gasket from leaking. A piece of thin aluminum is hand trimmed to fit the shape of the passages and is sealed in place with gasket contact adhesive. Nothing fancy is required here--in fact, Wilson uses aluminum beverage cans as the source of aluminum. The new style of Chevy angle plug heads does not have a carburetor heating passage.

The intake manifold gaskets are glued with Ford Gasket and Seal Contact Adhesive (Ford part number B9AE 19B508-A), and attached to the heads. This is the best type of adhesive Wilson has ever found. It keeps the gaskets in place when the manifold is laid down and shifted about for the best fit. This sealant is a **contact** adhesive, so it has to be applied to both objects being glued. Apply the adhesive in a thin, even layer. The gaskets are lined up as best as possible with the port openings, then if any gasket material protrudes into the ports, it is carefully trimmed out with a razor blade.

The Jomar stud girdle is used with the Chevrolet 350, and with the kit comes a spacer which is placed on the heads to move the valve covers upward for clearance. The Jomar kit spacer

After intake manifold gasket is cemented in place, a razor blade is used to trim away any gasket material which protrudes into the head ports.

A piece of aluminum is attached with contact cement over the heat riser passage. The aluminum was cut out of an old Coke can. This is the old style of Chevy angle plug head. The newest style has the passage blocked already in the casting.

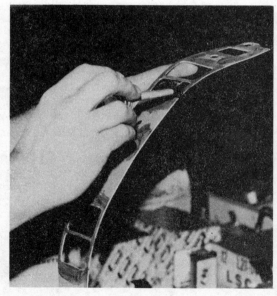

Intake manifold gasket is coated with Ford gasket contact adhesive before being fitted to head.

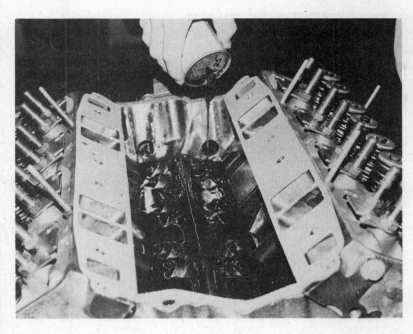

The GM EOS is poured liberally into the engine oil valley before the intake manifold is attached.

screws are discarded and replaced with 3" tall threaded studs, screwed into the heads. This allows the gaskets and spacers to be dropped over the studs for more precise alignment of them. The top and bottom gaskets are glued onto the spacer with contact adhesive before they are dropped into place on the heads.

The push rods being used in the Chevy 350 are the stock Chevrolet part. No matter what kind of push rods are being used, check them for straightness by rolling them on a flat surface. Stock push rods, especially, have a tendency to come out of the box slightly bent. It might be a good idea to make friends with a cooperative parts man so he will let you check a whole batch of push rods before you purchase them, then take a full set of straight ones. Do not ever attempt to staighten a push rod. You'd just be building in a stress point in an already highly stressed part. For non-stock lengths of push rods, Wilson relies on Crane parts.

The rocker arms (on Fords and Chevrolets) are oiled from inside the push rods, so be sure they are absolutely clean. Shoot oil down inside the push rods once they are installed. Also, check the push rods for sufficient clearance around the valley baffle.

INSTALLING THE INTAKE MANIFORD

The front and rear of the block is sealed with a cork--not a rubber--gasket. Rubber will compress with torque, but not necessarily seal. The corners of the cork gaskets at the ends of the block, where

they overlap the intake manifold gaskets, are trimmed on an angle with a razor blade to help sealing. The ends then get a small dab of silicone rubber sealant before the manifold goes on. After the manifold is attached, a small bead of silicone rubber is run along the manifold-gasket-block sealing edge to add extra insurance against oil leakage.

Once the manifold is set on the engine, use an

The intake manifold is set in place on top of gaskets which have already been glued in position.

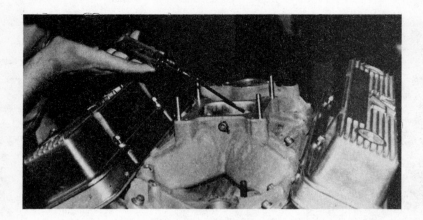

Wilson uses an examination light to be sure intake manifold runners are lined up exactly with head ports.

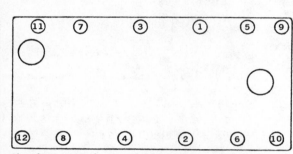

Chrysler 340 intake manifold torque sequence. The forward end of the manifold is at right.

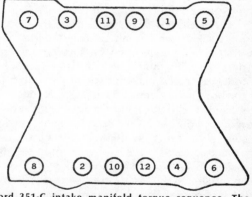

Chevy 350 intake manifold torque sequence. The forward end of the manifold is at left.

Ford 351-C intake manifold torque sequence. The forward end is at left.

inspection light to check down inside the port runners. Be sure the manifold ports are **perfectly** lined up with the head ports. The manifold can be shifted slightly for a better fit. Don't worry if the manifold ports are just a little smaller than the

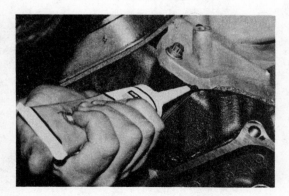

Front and rear sealing surfaces of intake manifold are sealed with Dow Corning silicone rubber to insure against leaks.

head openings—they are much better smaller than larger. Make sure you observe the proper torquing pattern sequence when securing the manifold.

INSTALLING THE ROCKER ARMS

The rocker arms being used on our sample Chevy 350 engine are the Crane 1.60 ratio needle bearing arms. The valley of the rocker arms are oiled after being installed on oiled rocker studs.

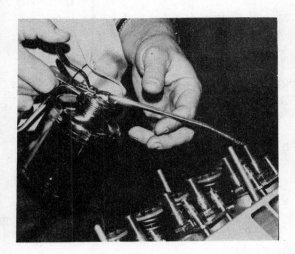

The rocker studs are oiled before the rocker arms are installed.

Oil filter is filled to capacity with Union 20W50 oil before being attached to block.

Make sure the round surface of the rocker stud nut is installed facing down and the flat surface is up. The nut can be installed and adjusted in the wrong position, but the nut will break if installed upside down.

Run the lash adjusting caps down finger tight, then back them off just a bit. Use a feeler gauge to set the lash to hot specs. Check for push rod bind once the arms are tightened. Then the Jomar stud girdle can be installed (be sure to oil the bolts on it).

Tighten the stud girdle bolts to 12 ft/lbs. They cannot be too tight because the aluminum stud girdle support bar expands as the engine heats up, tightening the bolts even more. When tightening the girdle bolts, start in the center first and work in a pattern outward.

The valves have to be adjusted first so there is a top surface to line the stud girdle up against. The distance from the top of the rocker lash cap to the top of the girdle bar should be .125".

Once the stud girdle is tightened, go back and check valve lash again. It could change from the girdle being tightened. The feeler gauge should feel snug when the lash is correct.

Finish the few remaining details on the engine, then install the carburetor. If the carburetor is not going to be installed until much later after the intake manifold is installed, tape up the carb opening so no debris can enter the engine. When installing the carburetor, look down through the throttle bores to be sure they line up with the manifold, and there are no restrictions.

The distributor is the last component to be installed. Do not install it until just before the engine is going to be fired up, so the oil pump can be manually primed.

MAJOR PART NUMBERS

Part	Chevy 350	MoPar 340	Ford 351-C
Cylinder block	GM # 366246	P 3690898	M-6051-A3
Cylinder head	GM # 3965784	MoPar 2531902 or P3870812 (W-2)	D1ZZ-6049-B or M-6049-A3 (aluminum)
Head gasket	GM # 3916336	P 3512719 (1) 3698659 (2)	D3ZZ-6051-A
Engine gasket set	GM # 3970634	P 3690174	Fel Pro FS 8347 PT and CS 8347
Crankshaft	GM # 3941184	2843868	M-6302-B351
Main bearings	TRW # MS 2909 P	TRW # MS 2963 P	TRW # MS 3010 P
Windage tray	GM # 3727136	MoPar # 2531945	None
Rear main oil seal	GM # 3958001	MoPar # 3577303	D00Z-6701-A
Vibration dampner	GM # 3817173	P 2532202	M-6316-A3
Timing chain	Cloyes # 9-3100 (gear set) 9-200 (wear plate)	Cloyes # 9-3103	Cloyes # 9-3121
Connecting rods	(3)	(3)	(3)
Connecting rod bearings	TRW # CB 663 P	P 3690684	TRW # CB 927 P
Pistons	(4)	(4)	(4)
Piston rings	Speed Pro R-9342	Speed Pro R-9600	Speed Pro R-9342
Intake valves	GM # 366285	MoPar # P 3690230	Manley 11810 or Ford #M-6507-D321
Exhaust valves	TRW # S 2699 H	MoPar # P 3690231	Manley 11811 or Ford #M-6505-D321
Valve seals	Perfect Circle	Perfect Circle	Perfect Circle
Tappets	TRW # VL 43	MoPar #P2843177	TRW # VL 48
Rocker arms	Crane # 11757 (6)	MoPar # 2806 988	Crane # 27750
Intake manifold	Edelbrock Victor	Edelbrock Victor 340	Edelbrock Torker
Oil pump	GM # 3969870	MoPar #P4286589	Ford #M-6600-C3

Water pump	6258551	3420038	D00Z-8501-C
Pushrods	3796243	P3690988	M-6565-A342
Push rod guides	3879620	N.A.	C9ZZ-6A564-A
Oil pump drive shaft	3865886	P 3690715	M-6605-A351
Spark plugs (general)	Champion BL-60	Champion N60R	Champion BL-60
Spark plug gap	025	.022	.025
Fuel pump	Carter M-4891	Carter	Carter M 4861 (5)

Notes:
(1) High performance steel gasket.
(2) Stock composition gasket
(3) See connecting rod chapter

(4) See Piston chapter.
(5) Bud Moore has a special 351-C fuel pump for Grand National racing.
(6) 1.6:1 ratio. For 1.5:1 ratio use #11756

CRITICAL TORQUE SPECIFICATIONS

Component	Chevy 350	Chrysler 340	Ford 351-C
Cylinder head bolts	70 — long bolts 60 — short bolts	100	120
Main bearing cap bolts	70 — long bolts 65 — short bolts	100 (center) 45 (outboard)	105 — 1/2" bolts 45 — 3/8" bolts
Connecting rod bolts	*	*	*
Intake manifold bolts	25	45	32 — 3/8" bolts 25 — 5/16" bolts
Spark plugs	15	30	15
Flywheel to crankshaft	60	55	80
Header bolts	25	20	20
Rocker arm mounting studs	50	25 (shaft screw)	75
Camshaft sprocket bolts	20	35	45

Note: All torque given in foot-pounds.

* Refer to rod manufacturer's specifications.

CRITICAL CLEARANCES

Component	Clearance
Piston to bore	.007*
Piston ring end gap	.015**
Piston to top of head	.040
Valve to piston intake	.080
Exhaust valve to piston	.100
Main bearing	.0025
Crankshaft end play	.007
Connecting rod bearing	.0025
Connecting rod side	.020
Piston pin in rod	.0008
Piston pin in piston	.0008
Piston pin end play	.000
Camshaft end play	.006
Tappet in block	.002
Intake valve stem (stock guide)	.0012
Exhaust valve stem (stock guide)	.003
Intake valve (bronze inserts)	.0002
Exhaust valve stem (bronze inserts)	.0002

* With Venolia pistons, use .009"-.010" clearance. Clearance noted is for TRW and Diamond pistons.

** For constant operation tracks like Daytona, use .017" on top ring and .015" on second ring.

Dyno Testing

The moment every engine builder waits for is the dyno testing of his new creation. It is on the dynamometer where he determines if everything is going to function properly, if there are any leaks or problems, and most importantly, what the torque and horsepower ratings are. If you do not want to leave anything to chance, it is essential you test each and every engine you use in competition on a dynamometer.

Only one component has to be run differently on a dyno than on the competition engine, and this is for a break-in procedure only. The valve springs should be run with the inner springs removed. This insures good break-in of the cam without excessive wear on the lobes. The first 30 minutes of running time on a new engine are the most critical on a new cam.

The last component to be installed on the engine before firing it up is the distributor. This is so the oil pump can be manually primed. Reach into the distributor bore with a speed handle wrench (with a slotted end) and rotate the oil pump until oil can be heard sloshing inside. Be sure the engine is already filled to capacity with new oil

To set the timing once the distributor is in, click the starter until the damper is at 12° BTDC (this is assuming the distributor is set with 13° advance and the desired total advance is 38°). Switch on the ignition, then turn the distributor by hand counter-clockwise (the reverse of its direction of travel) while holding the number one spark plug wire terminal just slightly away from a ground. When you observe a spark between the terminal and the ground, you have found the number one cylinder firing position of the distributor. At this point (do not let the distributor rotate past the firing point) clamp down the distributor securely. This will bring the timing to within a 1° to 2° accuracy.

WARM-UP PROCEDURE

The engine should be ready to go as soon as you fire it up. The oil pump should already be primed, and the carburetor and fuel line should already be primed with fuel.

For the dyno break-in and testing procedures, use a Champion BL-3 (or its equivalent heat range in another brand) spark plug. This warm plug will continue firing correctly even if it should become fouled.

Upon engine firing, bring it up to 2500 RPM immediately. Idling is bad for a new engine. Keep the RPMs at 2500 for 20 to 30 minutes. While the engine is running during its initial break-in, you will notice that the oil pressure will go down and the torque will increase. The RPMs will also increase in the first 3 to 5 minutes. This is normal as the friction inside the engine decreases

After 20-30 minutes, shut the engine off. Check the spark plugs for their color reading. Re-torque the heads, check the valve lash, check for oil and water leaks and check the timing. Then change

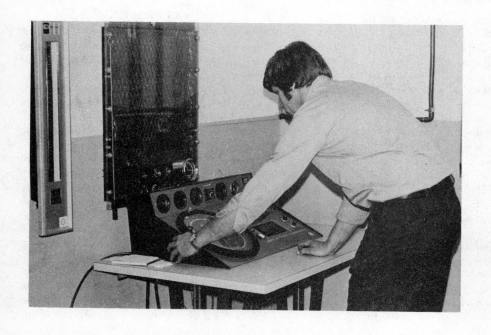

the oil filter. Any trash or lint in the engine will have been caught already. Don't take any chances of recirculating it back to the engine.

The next step is to install the inner valve springs so power runs can be made to determine the torque and horsepower output of the engine. When taking the rocker arms and lash caps off, check them over very closely for any failures or unusual wear marks. Keep all the rocker arms and stud girdle parts in order as they are disassembled so they can go back on the same cylinder once again.

With the headers removed look inside the exhaust ports to be sure the rings have seated. They should have seated after 30 minutes of break-in time.

ADJUSTING THE VALVES

The last procedure before the power runs are undertaken is the adjustment of the valves. Methods vary slightly from one mechanic to the next, but this is the procedure Wilson uses:

Start with the number one cylinder. When the number one exhaust valve just starts to open,

If the valve train assembly must be dismantled, as was the case when the inner valve springs were installed during dyno testing, all components are laid out in order so they can be reassembled as they came off engine.

adjust the intake valve on that cylinder. With the starter, tap the engine all the way through the intake open, and just as it begins closing, adjust the exhaust valve. Adjust both valves of one cylinder at a time. Taking the cylinders in firing order makes the job easier.

THE POWER RUNS

The power runs are accomplished by bringing the engine up to a specified RPM range, and while the operator holds it there, an observor records the torque reading from the scale on the dyno instrumentation. After the power runs have been completed, the torque is mathematically converted into horsepower with the following formula:

$$HP = \frac{Torque \times RPM}{5250}$$

All torque and horsepower figures have to be standardized to the SAE correction factor in order to be compared. This takes into account altitude and air temperature. The standard for comparison is an engine at sea level barometric pressure of 29.92 inches of mercury with air temperature at 60° F.

The power runs we recorded with the Chevrolet 350 we built for this book were:

Torque (ft/lbs)	RPM	Horsepower
435	4500	373
443	5000	422
447	5500	468
433	6000	495
413	6500	511
379	7000	506

One more instrument which dynamometers are equipped with is a pyrometer which instantly registers the temperature of the exhaust. It is extremely useful for checking cylinder distribution and air/fuel mixture. The ideal temperature for a competition engine cylinder is 1350° to 1400°F. Anything higher indicates an over-lean condition. If the engine is under that temperature, an over-rich condition is present. The probe of the pyrometer is inserted into a small hole (usually about 3/32") in each header pipe, drilled about 1½" from the header flange.

The last instrument you will find on a dynamometer is a fuel flow meter. It measures the amount of fuel, in pounds per hour, which the engine requires to make the torque and horsepower which are being recorded. The fuel flow is divided by the corrected horsepower and a number called the "brake specific" is the result. A chart of the brake specific through the testing RPM range will give an indication of how efficiently the engine is making power. Generally, the brake specific curve should be very flat and be as low as possible (at least under .47). The brake specific can be used to pinpoint specific areas in the engine which are hurting the power output. For example, if the torque is good, but corrected horsepower is down and the brake specific is up, the problem will generally be with the camshaft or headers. If the horsepower is down, the torque is stable and the brake specific is lean, then cylinder head breathing ability and/or piston dome config-uration may be suspected.

The easiest way to understand the testing procedures on a dyno and the information which can be learned from it is to examine the results of an actual testing program. The following results are from a Chevrolet 350 Grand National engine built by Waddell Wilson which we used for experimental purposes. The specifications of the engine being tested: 4.00" bore, 3.55" stroke, 6.00" rods, TRW pistons, CHA modified heads, TRW valves, Edelbrock Scorpion intake manifold, Holley 830 CFM carburetor, Reed cam (314° duration intake and exhaust, .387" lobe lift, 102° overlap, 106° lobe centers) and Crane 1.6 to 1 ratio rocker arms. The engine had 400 miles of superspeedway racing on it before being installed on the dyno, which greatly affected the condition of the heads. Following are the test results:

Test #1
This test was run on the engine to establish a baseline.

RPM	HP	Brake Specific
5000	385	.500
5500	425	.511
6000	460	.514
6500	478	.541
7000	476	.567

Comments: The horsepower figure is disappointing. The higher than normal brake specific indicates the jetting is too rich.

Change: The carburetor was rejetted with 85s in the primaries and 84s in the secondaires. The carburetor previously had 90s in the primaries and 89 in the secondaries. A one-inch tall open spacer was also added under the carburetor.

Test #2

RPM	HP	Brake Specific
5000	388	.449
5500	425	.459
6000	469	.461
6500	488	.469
7000	489	.493

Comments: The brake specific looks much better. It and the increased horsepower indicate the small block engine likes to run lean.

Change: Add one more 1″ tall open spacer under the carburetor.

Test #3

RPM	HP	Brake Specific
5000	389	.444
5500	431	.443
6000	469	.461
6500	485	.471
7000	492	.487

Comments: The brake specific shows that the spacer increased the leanness of the fuel/air mixture. This was actually because the spacer increased the velocity of the mixture entering the engine. This also increased power output. After the third run, the heads were removed to inspect their condition. Evidence of a bad reversion problem was found in the heads and intake manifold. The heads also showed bad wear on the seat angles and valve faces. This definitely has an effect on the breathing ability of the heads.

Change: New heads were installed with new valve job.

Test #4

RPM	HP	Brake Specific
5000	387	.442
5500	432	.444
6000	480	.453
6500	503	.456
7000	511	.464

Change: Advance cam 4°.

Test #5

RPM	HP	Brake Specific
5000	393	.445
5500	438	.436
6000	481	.441
6500	504	.442
7000	509	.495

Comment: This change created more power in the lower RPM range and hurt the top end slightly.

Change: New Reed cam. All specifications identical to previous cam except lobe lift higher at .391″ and 108° lobe displacement center.

Test #6

RPM	HP	Brake Specific
5000	389	.445
5500	432	.449
6000	475	.444
6500	500	.463
7000	507	.480

Comments: The power was off through the entire range, but the brake specific looked very good. Through previous experience with the cam which was installed, it was known that the cam should have increased horsepower. This led Wilson to believe the problem was in engine breathing ability. The intake manifold was removed and evidence of severe reversion was discovered. The problem, Wilson felt, was that someone had modified the runner configuration of the manifold by grinding in it. To check, a new Scorpion manifold, with only the casting imperfections cleaned from the interior of the runners, was installed. No other changes were made.

Test #7

RPM	HP	Brake Specific
5000	393	.432
5500	439	.434
6000	485	.432
6500	510	.439
7000	519	.452

Comments: The horsepower was up significantly and the brake specific was down and very flat (very little change through the RPM range). The engine's most serious roadblock to making power was its ability to breathe properly because of reversion.

Change: All tests prior to this have been carried out with the dynomometer headers installed. Now tests for the correct header combination are carried out since the right cam, manifold and head combinations have been determined. Stahl headers were installed, 17/8" diameter primary pipes, 32" long.

Test #8

RPM	HP	Brake Specific
5000	385	.452
5500	432	.438
6000	476	.443
6500	504	.474
7000	510	.496

Change: 3" diameter crossover pipe was installed in secondary header pipes just behind collectors.

Test #9

RPM	HP	Brake Specific
5000	398	.445
5500	452	.438
6000	486	.424
6500	505	.467
7000	511	.481

Comments: The crossover pipe significantly brought the horsepower up, but the brake specific was very erratic, indicating that the engine still is not breathing properly.

Change: Kustom headers installed. 1-7/8" OD primary pipes, 34" long. Crossover pipe was retained.

Test #10

RPM	HP	Brake Specific
5000	398	.437
5500	446	.434
6000	488	.441
6500	508	.460
7000	513	.475

Comments: The brake specific still varies too much, so the correct scavenging system for the exhaust still has not been found.

Change: Kustom 17/8" OD headers with 36" long primary pipes.

Test #11

RPM	HP	Brake Specific
5000	402	.447
5500	452	.433
6000	486	.456
6500	508	.454
7000	509	.471

Change: Hooker 1-7/8" OD headers, 38" long primary pipes.

Test #12

RPM	HP	Brake Specific
5000	397	.443
5500	447	.431
6000	490	.444
6500	508	.448
7000	515	.474

Comments: The Hooker headers showed a great improvement in the exhaust gas scavenging and the entire flow velocity. They helped the top end best.

Cylinder Displacement Table

NOTE: This chart has been compiled to easily calculate engine displacement from known bore and stroke sizes. Cubic centimeters may also be determined by conversion shown. To obtain total displacement, multiply box figure by number of cylinders. EXAMPLE: Ford, 4.00″ bore x 2.87 stroke = 36.06. 36.06 x 8 = 289 cu. in. To convert cubic inches to cubic centimeters divide box figure by .061.

Stroke	Bore 3½	3-9/16	3⅝	3-11/16	3¾	3-13/16	3⅞	3-15/16	4.00	4-1/16	4⅛	4-3/16	4¼	4-5/16	4⅜
2.5	24.05	24.91	25.80	26.69	27.61	28.53	29.48	30.44	31.41	32.40	33.41	34.43	35.46	36.51	37.58
2.6	25.01	25.90	26.83	27.75	28.71	29.67	30.66	31.65	32.67	33.70	34.74	35.80	36.88	37.97	39.08
2.7	25.97	26.90	27.86	28.82	29.82	30.81	31.84	32.87	33.92	34.99	36.08	37.18	38.30	39.43	40.58
2.8	26.93	27.90	28.89	29.89	30.92	31.95	33.02	34.09	35.18	36.29	37.41	38.56	39.72	40.89	42.09
2.87	27.61	28.59	29.62	30.64	31.69	32.75	33.84	34.94	36.06	37.20	38.35	39.52	40.71	41.92	43.14
2.94	28.28	29.29	30.34	31.38	32.47	33.55	34.67	35.79	36.94	38.10	39.29	40.48	41.70	42.94	44.19
3.00	28.86	29.89	30.96	32.03	33.13	34.23	35.37	36.53	37.69	38.88	40.09	41.31	42.55	43.81	45.09
3.10	29.82	30.89	31.99	33.09	34.23	35.38	36.55	37.74	38.95	40.18	41.42	42.69	43.97	45.28	46.60
3.20	30.78	31.89	33.02	34.16	35.34	36.52	37.73	38.96	40.21	41.47	42.76	44.07	45.39	46.74	48.10
3.25	31.26	32.38	33.54	34.69	35.89	37.09	38.32	39.57	40.84	42.12	43.43	44.75	46.10	47.47	48.85
3.30	31.74	32.88	34.05	35.23	36.44	37.66	38.91	40.18	41.46	42.77	44.40	45.44	46.81	48.20	49.60
3.38	32.51	33.68	34.88	36.08	37.33	38.57	39.86	41.15	42.47	43.81	45.17	46.54	47.94	49.39	50.81
3.40	32.71	33.88	33.09	36.30	37.55	38.80	40.09	41.40	42.72	44.07	45.43	46.82	48.23	49.66	51.11
3.44	33.09	34.27	35.50	36.72	37.99	39.26	40.56	41.88	43.22	44.58	45.97	47.37	48.80	50.24	51.71
3.50	33.67	34.87	36.12	37.36	38.65	39.94	41.27	42.61	43.98	45.36	46.77	48.20	49.65	51.12	52.61
3.56	34.25	35.47	36.74	38.00	39.31	40.62	41.98	43.34	44.73	46.14	47.57	49.02	50.50	51.99	53.51
3.60	34.63	35.87	37.15	38.43	39.76	41.08	42.45	43.83	45.23	46.66	48.11	49.57	51.07	52.58	54.11
3.62	34.82	36.07	37.36	38.64	39.98	41.31	42.69	44.07	45.49	46.92	48.37	49.85	51.35	52.87	54.41
3.64	35.02	36.27	37.56	38.86	40.20	41.54	42.92	44.32	45.74	47.18	48.64	50.13	51.63	53.16	54.72
3.66	33.21	36.47	37.77	39.07	40.42	41.77	43.16	44.56	45.99	47.44	48.91	50.40	51.92	53.46	55.02
3.68	35.40	36.67	37.97	39.29	40.64	41.99	43.39	44.81	46.24	47.70	49.17	50.68	52.20	53.75	55.32
3.69	35.50	36.77	38.08	39.39	40.75	42.11	43.51	44.93	46.37	47.83	49.31	50.81	52.34	53.89	55.47
3.70	35.59	36.87	38.18	39.50	40.86	42.22	43.63	45.05	46.49	47.95	49.44	50.95	52.48	54.04	55.62
3.75	36.07	37.36	38.70	40.03	41.41	42.79	44.22	45.66	47.12	48.60	50.11	51.64	53.19	54.77	56.37
3.78	36.36	37.66	39.01	40.35	41.74	43.14	44.57	46.02	47.50	48.99	50.51	52.05	53.62	55.21	56.82
3.84	36.56	37.86	39.21	40.57	41.96	43.36	44.81	46.27	47.75	49.25	50.78	52.33	53.90	55.50	57.12
3.87	37.23	38.56	39.94	41.31	42.74	44.16	45.63	47.12	48.63	50.16	51.71	53.29	54.90	56.52	58.17
3.90	37.52	38.86	40.25	41.63	43.07	44.51	45.99	47.48	49.00	50.55	52.11	53.71	55.32	56.96	58.62
3.94	37.90	39.26	40.66	42.06	43.51	44.96	46.46	47.97	49.51	51.07	52.65	54.26	55.89	57.54	59.23
4.00	38.48	39.86	41.28	42.70	44.17	45.65	47.17	48.70	50.26	51.84	53.45	55.08	56.74	58.42	60.13

DECIMAL EQUIVALENTS

DRILL SIZE	DECIMAL	DRILL SIZE	DECIMAL	DRILL SIZE	DECIMAL	DRILL SIZE	DECIMAL
1/64	.0156	7/64	.1094	15/64	.2344	7/16	.4375
80	.0135	35	.1100	B	.2380	29/64	.4531
79	.0145	34	.1110	C	.2420	15/32	.4688
78	.0160	33	.1130	D	.2460	31/64	.4844
77	.0180	32	.1160	1/4	.2500	1/2	.5000
76	.0200	31	.1200	F	.2570	33/64	.5156
75	.0210	1/8	.1250	G	.2610	17/32	.5313
74	.0225	30	.1285	17/64	.2656	35/64	.5469
73	.0240	29	.1360	H	.2660	9/16	.5625
72	.0250	28	.1405	I	.2720	37/64	.5781
71	.0260	9/64	.1406	J	.2770	19/32	.5938
70	.0280	27	.1440	K	.2810	39/64	.6094
69	.0292	26	.1470	9/32	.2812	5/8	.6250
68	.0310	25	.1495	L	.2900	41/64	.6406
1/32	.0312	24	.1520	M	.2950	21/32	.6562
67	.0320	23	.1540	19/64	.2969	43/64	.6719
66	.0330	5/32	.1562	N	.3020	11/16	.6875
65	.0350	22	.1570	5/16	.3125	45/64	.7031
64	.0360	21	.1590	O	.3160	23/32	.7188
63	.0370	20	.1610	P	.3230	47/64	.7344
62	.0380	19	.1660	21/64	.3281	3/4	.7500
61	.0390	18	.1695	Q	.3320	49/64	.7656
60	.0400	11/64	.1719	R	.3390	25/32	.7812
59	.0410	17	.1730	11/32	.3438	51/64	.7969
58	.0420	16	.1770	S	.3480	13/16	.8125
57	.0430	15	.1800	T	.3580	53/64	.8281
56	.0465	14	.1820	23/64	.3594	27/32	.8438
3/64	.0469	13	.1850	U	.3680	55/64	.8594
55	.0520	3/16	.1875	3/8	.3750	7/8	.8750
54	.0550	12	.1890	V	.3770	57/64	.8906
53	.0595	11	.1910	W	.3860	29/32	.9062
1/16	.0625	10	.1935	25/64	.3906	59/64	.9219
52	.0635	9	.1960	X	.3970	15/16	.9375
51	.0670	8	.1990	Y	.4040	61/64	.9531
50	.0700	7	.2010	13/32	.4062	31/32	.9688
49	.0730	13/64	.2031	Z	.4130	64/64	.9844
48	.0760	6	.2040	27/64	.4219	1	1.000
5/64	.0781	5	.2055				
47	.0785	4	.2090				
46	.0810	3	.2130				
45	.0820	7/32	.2187				
44	.0860	2	.2210				
43	.0890	1	.2280				
42	.0935	A	.2340				
3/32	.0937						
41	.0960						
40	.0980						
39	.0995						
38	.1015						
37	.1040						
36	.1065						

TAP DRILL SIZES

THREAD	DRILL	THREAD	DRILL
0-80	3/64	1/2-20	29/64
1-64	NO. 53	9/16-12	31/64
1-72	NO. 53	9/16-18	33/64
2-56	NO. 50	5/8-11	17/32
2-64	NO. 51	5/8-18	37/64
3-48	NO. 47	3/4-10	21/32
3-56	NO. 45	3/4-16	11/16
4-40	NO. 43	7/8-9	49/64
4-48	NO. 42	7/8-14	13/16
5-40	NO. 38	1-8	7/8
5-44	NO. 37	1-12	59/64
6-32	NO. 36	1-14	15/16
6-40	NO. 33		
8-32	NO. 29		
8-36	NO. 29		
10-24	NO. 25		
10-32	NO. 21		
12-24	NO. 16		
12-28	NO. 14		
1/4-20	NO. 7		
1/4-28	NO. 3		
5/16-18	F		
5/16-24	I		
3/8-16	5/16		
3/8-24	Q		
7/16-14	U		
7/16-20	25/64		
1/2-13	27/64		

TAPER PIPE

THREAD	DRILL
1/8-27	R
1/4-18	7/16
3/8-18	37/64
1/2-14	45/64
3/4-14	59/64
1-11 1/2	1-5/32

STRAIGHT PIPE

THREAD	DRILL
1/8-27	11/32
1/4-18	7/16
3/8-18	37/64
1/2-14	23/32
3/4-14	59/64
1-11 1/2	1-5/32

SHEET METAL SCREW SIZES

DIAMETER	#4	#6	#7	#8	#10	#12	#14	5/16	3/8
DRILL SIZE	1/16	3/32	7/64	1/8	9/64	11/64	13/64	15/64	5/16

PIPE THREAD SIZES

1/8   1/4   3/8   1/2

Part Sources

The following addresses and phone numbers cover all of the parts suppliers we mention throughout the book. If you have a question about the price, application or availability of any part they make, please refer your questions to them. They will be very glad to help you. They will also be pleased to supply you with their current catalog, but be prepared to pay at least $1.00 for a catalog from any manufacturer. This is common and accepted practice in the automotive industry.

Brodix Heads
3021 S. 32nd Street
Ft. Smith, AR 72903
(501) 783-3251
   Aluminum heads

Autotronic Controls
6908 Commerce
El Paso, TX 79915
(915) 772-7431
   MSD ignition systems

Carrillo Connecting Rods
Warren Machine
33041 Calle Perfecto
San Juan Capistrano, CA. 92675
(714) 493-1230
   Connecting rods

Chrysler Performance Parts
P.O. Box 1081
Warren, MI 48090
(313) 497-5253
   MoPar "P" parts

Cloyes Gear and Products
17214 Roseland Rd.
Cleveland, OH. 44112
(216) 531-3261
   Timing gears and chains

Jack Cotten Ignitions
2115 Red Bluff
Pasadena, TX 77506
(713) 472-8874
   Ignition wiring and parts

Crane Cams Inc.
100 N.W. Ninth Terrace
Hallandale, FL. 33009
(315) 457-8888
   Cams

Crankshaft Co.
1422 S. Main St.
Los Angeles, CA. 90015
(213) 749-6597
   Crankshafts, connecting rods

Crower Cam and Equipment Co.
3333 Main St.
Chula Vista, CA. 92011
(619) 422-1178
   Cams, connecting rods

Diamond Racing
3493 Ten Mile Rd.
Warren, MI 48091
(313) 756-4055

Edelbrock Equipment Co.
411 Coral Circle
El Segundo, CA. 90245
(213) 322-7310
   Intake manifolds

Mr. Gasket Co.
4566 Spring Rd.
Brooklyn Heights, OH. 44131
(216) 398-8300
   Gaskets, Jomar stud girdles, ignition parts

Holley Carburetors
11955 E. Nine Mile Rd.
Warren, MI. 48090
(313) 536-1900
   Carburetors

Hooker Headers
1032 W. Brooks St.
Ontario, CA. 91762
(714) 983-5871
   Headers

Iskenderian Cams
16020 S. Broadway
Gardena, CA. 90248
(213) 770-0930
   Cams

Jomar Engineering Co.
1841 Thunderbird
Troy, MI 48084
(313) 362-2830
   Valve train stud girdles

Offenhauser Equipment Co.
5300 Alhambra Ave.
Los Angeles, CA 90032
(213) 225-1307
   Intake manifolds

Ross Racing Pistons
11927 S. Prairie
Hawthorne, CA 90250
(213) 644-9779

Reed Cams
Bldg. 35-B, Peachtree-DeKalb Airport
Chamblee, GA 30341
(404) 451-5086
   Cams, cylinder head modification

Speed Pro/Sealed Power
2001 Sanford St.
Muskegon, MI 49443
(616) 726-3261
   Rings, pistons, valve train parts

Junior Johnson Associates
Rte. 2, Box 86
Ronda, NC 28670
(919) 984-2101
   Dry sump oil adaptors, belt pulleys, dry break
   fueling systems

Blum's Racing Ent.
3111 S. Valley View, #B-110
Las Vegas, NV 89102
(702) 871-8115
   Wet and dry sump oil pans

Mallory Electric Corp.
1801 Oregon St.
Carson City, NV 89701
(702) 882-6600
   Ignition equipment

Manley Performance Engineering
13 Race St.
Bloomfield, NJ 07003
(201) 743-6577
   Valve train equipment

Milodon Engineering
9134 Independence
Chatsworth, CA 91311
(818) 882-4727
   Oil pans, oiling equipment, main caps

Ford Motorsport Performance Equip.
17000 Southfield Road
Allen Park, MI 48101
(313) 323-5356

Moldex Tool Co.
25249 W. Warren Ave.
Dearborn Heights, MI 48127
(313) 561-7676
   Forged crankshafts

Bud Moore Engineering
400 N. Fairview
Spartanburg, SC 29302
(803) 585-8155
   351-C intake manifolds and parts

Moroso Performance Sales
Carter Dr.
Guilford, CT 06437
(203) 453-6571
   Oil pans and equipment

Stahl Headers
1515 Mt. Rose Ave.
York, PA 17403
(717) 846-1632
   Headers

TRW Performance Parts
8001 E. Pleasant Valley Rd.
Cleveland, OH 44131
   Pistons, valves, bearings

Venolia Pistons
2160 Cherry Industrial Circle
Long Beach, CA 90805
(213) 636-9329
   Forged pistons

Borg Warner Automotive Parts
11045 Gage Ave.
Franklin Park, IL 60131
   Ignition parts, clutches, transmissions

Weaver Brothers Ltd.
1980 Boeing Way
Carson City, NV
(702) 883-7677
   Dry sump systems

Weiand Racing Equipment
2737 San Fernando Rd.
Los Angeles, CA 90065
(213) 225-4138
   Intake manifolds

Yother Performance Products
616 Doolittle Dr.
San Leandro, CA 94577
(415) 632-9913
   Honing plates

BOLT TORQUE SPECIFICATIONS

Bolt Diameter	Threads per Inch	SAE Grade					
		5[1]		7[2]		8[3]	
		Torque[4]					
		Dry	Oiled	Dry	Oiled	Dry	Oiled
1/4	20	8	6-1/4	10	8	12	9
1/4	28	10	7-1/8	12	9	14	10
5/16	18	17	13	21	16	25	18
5/16	24	19	14	24	18	25	20
3/8	16	30	23	40	30	45	35
3/8	24	35	25	45	30	50	35
7/16	14	50	35	60	45	70	55
7/16	20	55	40	70	50	80	60
1/2	13	75	55	95	70	110	80
1/2	20	90	65	100	80	120	90
9/16	12	110	80	135	100	150	110
9/16	18	120	90	150	110	170	130
5/8	11	150	110	140	140	220	170
5/8	18	180	130	210	160	240	180
3/4	10	260	200	320	240	380	280
3/4	16	300	220	360	280	420	320
7/8	9	430	320	520	400	600	460
7/8	14	470	360	580	440	600	500
1	8	640	480	800	600	900	680
1	12	710	530	860	666	1000	740

(1) Grade 5 bolts have a tensile strength of 120,000 PSI, and have three slash marks on the heads.

(2) Grade 7 bolts have a tensile strength of 133,000 PSI, and have five slash marks on the head.

(3) Grade 8 bolts have a tensile strength of 150,000 PSI and have six slash marks on the head.

(4) All torque is in foot-pounds.

Notes

Engine Building Log

DATE	TYPE OF SERVICE	COST	REMARKS

Engine Building Log

DATE	TYPE OF SERVICE	COST	REMARKS

Engine Building Log

DATE	TYPE OF SERVICE	COST	REMARKS

Engine Building Log

DATE	TYPE OF SERVICE	COST	REMARKS

Other books from Steve Smith Autosports

If you have enjoyed **Racing Engine Preparation**, we invite you to investigate Steve Smith Autosports' other publications. All are professionally written with expert, easy-to-understand text, and fully illustrated. To order any book listed, specify book number and send full price plus **$1** per book handling to Steve Smith Autosports, P.O. Box 11631, Santa Ana, CA 92711.

Building The Hobby Stock/Street Stock Car

By Bob Emmons

This book is written for the low-buck racer with limited facilities and who wants to farm out a minimum of work. It shows you how to build a car with a minimum of "store-bought" parts of expensive machine work. Chapters include: your choice of car • cage construction • chassis vs. unitized car • engine, cooling and electrics • transmissions and rear ends • tires and wheels • suspension (parts choice, building and sorting) • driving • spare parts and preparation. For dirt and asphalt applications. **#S126 . . . $8.45**

Race Car Fabrication & Preparation

By Steve Smith

Includes thorough discussion of: prepping a transmission • setting up the rear end • electrical system • building the chassis and roll cage • cutting costs and beating the economy stock rules • welding • clutches • safety systems • wrecking yard parts • fabrication • hardware • wheels and tires • cooling system • plumbing • driveshaft • Plus much, much more. Photo packed, over 160 pages. **#S114 . . . $9.95**

Stalking The Motorsports Sponsor

By Pat Bentley

The methods in this clear, precise book will help you set up a sponsorship program whether you race on a local, regional or national scale. **Yes, you** can do it! Includes details of what has worked for others, and how you can duplicate the success. **#S119 . . . $7.95**

Racer's Complete Reference Guide

This book is the "Yellow Pages" of the high performance world. Tells you who makes it and where to find it for parts, hardware, services, anything. Says **Stock Car Racing Magazine** "The book is a handy guide to the makers and suppliers of parts and services. This book's a bible you can't be without!" New revised edition just released. **#S108 . . . $7.95**

Stock Car Driving Techniques

By Benny Parsons

Written with detail and authority by 1975 Daytona 500 winner Benny Parsons. Chapters include: Basic competition techniques • getting started in racing • developing a proper driving style • driving the dirt • improving your lap times • defensive driving techniques • super speedway driving details. Covers every aspect of competition driving. 96 pages. **#S104 . . . $7.95**

Dirt Track Chassis Technology

By Steve Smith

A dynamite source book for the changing, and most innovative form of racing. A nuts-and-bolts discussion of every facet of dirt track racing, including: specific chassis set-up recommendations • how to judge and adjust for a changing track • side bite • leaf spring vs. coil spring • proper weight distribution • details of the new 5-spring coil/over suspension • tires • shock absorbers • front and rear suspension systems • chassis construction • aerodynamics • preparation tips, plus much, much more. Packed with helpful photos and diagrams, plus the best state-of-the-art racing information. For the veteran or novice, a book you shouldn't be without. **#S133 . . . $10.95**

Sprint Car Technology

By Don Alexander

A complete book on buying, building and racing a sprinter, midget or super modified. It includes an in-depth study of current chassis design and components, and all the elements required to make a competitive race car. Chapters include: chassis structure • torsion bars — theory — parallel vs. cross — stocked vs. level • straight front axles • live axle rear • De Dion rear • bird cages • lateral locating linkages • steering layout • bump steer • king pin inclination • shocks • roll, roll couple and roll centers • side bite • braking • tires • dirt vs. asphalt set-ups and more. **#S125 . . . $9.95**

The Racer's Tax Guide

By Steve Smith

How to save BIG money on your racing activities. This book tells you how to LEGALLY subtract your racing costs from your income tax bill by running your operation like a business and following 3 simple steps. An alternative form of funding your racing. Includes a concise, up-to-the-minute report on how the new tax laws and changes help you save even MORE money. Read this book **now** and start saving! It works! **#S116 . . . $8.95**

Race Car Graphics

By Gary Smith

Takes the "magic" out of race car coloring, painting, numbering, striping, graphic design, etc. It shows you how to make your car and operation look absolutely professional without spending a lot of time and money. Author Gary Smith knows his field — he has designed a number of SCCA and IMSA race cars and two Indy 500 pace cars. 8 pages of full color photos. **#S118 . . . $7.95**

Stock Car Chassis Technology

By Steve Smith

The latest in race car suspension tips. Presents all the newest ideas in stock car chassis set-up. This book is all about how to put theory into practice. Includes: chassis set-up principles — procedure for set-up at the shop, actual case studies, troubleshooting the chassis, dialing in a new car, testing • front suspension principles, set-up and adjustment • choosing the right parts for your type of racing • rear suspension — all the new systems, torque absorbing devices, torque arms, locating devices • savings weight — building a lightweight car that's practical • the ideal car — design criteria • repairing a crashed chassis • the 50 most-asked questions • aerodynamics • and much, much more. Filled with photos and drawings. No complicated math or formulas — just easy-to-understand, practical information to make you more competitive. **#S139 . . . $12.95˙**

Advanced Race Car Suspension Development

By Steve Smith

The latest technological information about race car suspension design and development. A former GM chassis engineer reviewed it: "This is the most complete and accurate suspension book ever published."

The book details everything about race car suspension design, dynamic chassis analysis, chassis structure, handling stability and testing techniques. 176 pages, over 100 photos and drawings. #S105 . . . $8.45

Workbook For Advanced Race Car Suspension

The Work Book extracts all formulas presented in the parent book and treats them in a point-by-point manner to follow as examples of a complete chassis analysis. Includes updated material. An indispensible guide. #WB5 $5.45

The Racer's Tax Guide

By Steve Smith

How to save BIG money on your racing activities. This book tells you how to LEGALLY subtract your racing costs from your income tax bill by running your operation like a business and following 3 simple steps. An alternative form of funding your racing. Includes a concise, up-to-the-minute report on how the new tax laws and changes help you save even MORE money. Read this book **now** and start saving! It works! #S116 . . . $8.95

Engine Builder's Notebook

An 8-page booklet you can use to store all your information and specs for each engine you build. Lists every engine building step in correct order. A real frustration saver. #S121 . . . $4.95

Chevy Heavy Duty Parts List

By John Thawley

It is up-to-date with all of the newest stuff from the factory. Complete with all engine and drive-line goodies, plus much more miscellaneous info for the racer. Includes all high performance parts for the Chevy V6. Updated January 1983. #S120 . . . $4.95

Buick Free Spirit Power Manual

By John Thawley

Complete information on the performance engine of the future — the Buick V6. Blocks, crankshafts, rods, valve gear, intake and exhaust systems, ignition, suspension, brakes and body modifications. Includes chapter on building an IMSA Skyhawk. Complete list of performance hardware. Over 200 photos and drawings. #S123 . . . $8.95

Building The Chevy Sprint Car Engine

By John Thawley

The complete world of building a small block Chevy for a sprinter is detailed in this all new book. Includes complete info on the new Donovan and Milodon aluminum blocks, the Barnes Aluminum heads, injectors, burning alcohol. Engine building tips from the World of Outlaw competitors. Complete chapters on rods, cranks, valve train, the fuel injection system and magnetos. Dozens of tips on keeping the engine alive through night after night of dirt throwing action! More than 200 photos and drawings. #S130 . . . $8.95